THE COMMON LAW LIBRARY

McGREGOR

ON

DAMAGES

Second Supplement
to the
Seventeenth Edition

Up-to-date to beginning of August 2005

BY

HARVEY McGREGOR

Q.C., D.C.L., S.J.D.

CHAPTER 42 ON THE HUMAN RIGHTS ACT
BY MARTIN SPENCER Q.C.

CHAPTERS 43–45 ON PROCEDURE
BY JULIAN PICTON

LONDON
SWEET & MAXWELL
2005

Published in 2005 by
Sweet & Maxwell Limited of
100 Avenue Road, London NW3 3PF
(http://www.sweetandmaxwell.co.uk)
Typeset by
J&L Composition, Filey
North Yorkshire
Printed and bound in Great Britain by
Athenaeum Press Ltd., Gateshead, Tyne & Wear

No natural forests were destroyed to make this product.
Only farmed timber was used and replanted.

A catalogue record for this book is available from the British Library

ISBN Main Work 0–421–840 20X

ISBN First Supplement 0–421–861 800

ISBN Second Supplement 0–421–906 103

HOW TO USE THIS SUPPLEMENT

This is the Second Supplement to the Seventeenth Edition of
McGregor on Damages, and has been compiled according to the
structure of the main volume.

At the beginning of each chapter of this Supplement the mini table
of contents from the main volume has been included. Where a heading
in this table of contents has been marked with a square pointer, this
indicates that there is relevant information in the Supplement to which
the reader should refer. Material that is new to the Cumulative
Supplement is indicated by the symbol ■. Material that has been
included from the previous Supplement is indicated by the symbol □.

Within each chapter, updating information is referenced to
the relevant paragraph in the main volume.

HOW TO USE THIS SUPPLEMENT

This is the Second Supplement to the Seventeenth Edition of McGregor on Damages and has been compiled according to the structure of the main volume.

At the beginning of each chapter of this Supplement the usual table of contents from the main volume has been reproduced. Where a heading in this table of contents has been marked with a square pointer this indicates that there is relevant information in the Supplement to which the reader should refer. Material that is new to the Cumulative Supplement is indicated by the symbol ■. Material that has been included from the previous Supplement is indicated by the symbol □.

Within each chapter, updating information is referenced to the relevant paragraph in the main volume.

CONTENTS

BOOK TWO
PARTICULAR CLAIMS

BOOK THREE
PROCEDURE

TABLE OF CASES

TABLE OF STATUTES

TABLE OF STATUTORY INSTRUMENTS

TABLE OF CIVIL PROCEDURE RULES

BOOK ONE
GENERAL PRINCIPLES

DEFINITION, SCOPE, OBJECT AND TERMINOLOGY

1. DEFINITION OF THE TERM DAMAGES

(1) *Pecuniary compensation*

Insert a new note after the first sentence of the paragraph: **1–002**

NOTE 1a: Lord Hoffmann's comments in *The Gleaner Co Ltd v Abrahams* [2004] 1 A.C. 628, PC at para.41 that compensatory damages may be considered as fulfilling the dual function of compensation and of punishment, deterrence or example, and that this is an entirely orthodox view of such damages, are to be treated with caution. There is no doubt that the size of the award against an intentional tortfeasor may very effectively punish him and deter, and be an example to others, but this is purely *incidental* to the compensation for which the award is aiming. This situation can particularly arise with defamation, with which *Gleaner* was concerned, since the objects of damages are threefold rather than twofold, being not only compensation for pecuniary loss resulting from the defamation and for non-pecuniary loss from injury to feelings but also, as Lord Hoffmann pointed out at *ibid.*, para.55 (quoted at para.39–027, below), compensation by way of vindication of the claimant in the eyes of the world which generally calls for a sizable sum. Lord Hoffmann's comments had been prompted by his having to deal with the contention that Forte P. in the Jamaican Court of Appeal had misunderstood the distinction between exemplary and compensatory damages when he said that he considered that the very high amount of Jamaican dollars which the court was awarding, equivalent at the time to over half a million pounds, was sufficient to achieve the purpose of punishing the defendant and deterring others. Since this was said in the context of the claimant's unsuccessful cross-appeal from the trial court's refusal to award him exemplary damages, it is clear that what Forte P. had in mind was Lord Devlin's rule from the landmark *Rookes v Barnard* [1964] A.C. 1129, 1228, quoted at para.11–039 of the main text, that only if the amount being awarded for compensation was inadequate to punish and deter should exemplary damages be considered. It is also clear that Lord Hoffmann so interpreted Forte P. since he himself quoted Lord Devlin's rule: see on all this *Gleaner* at paras 40 and 41. Thus while Lord Hoffmann may say that, though Lord Hailsham in *Broome v Cassell & Co* [1972] A.C. 1027, 1077 regarded compensatory and exemplary damages as incompatible as oil and vinegar, "most judges have accepted that in many cases the two purposes are inextricably mixed" (*Gleaner* para.42), it is the compensatory purpose that is controlling. Skilfully and elegantly addressing Lord Hailsham's view later in the judgment, Lord Hoffmann pointed out that, though "oil and vinegar may not mix in solution . . . they combine to make an acceptable salad dressing" (*ibid.*, para.54). But it is the oil that matters and not the vinegar.

(2) *Tort or breach of contract*

(a) Money claims which are not based upon a tort or breach of contract but are not actions for damages

1–008   NOTE 8: For para.27–027 read para.29–007.

1–009   NOTE 9: Add at the end: For the possibility of aggravated damages in equity under Lord Cairns' Act see *Cardwell v Walker* [2004] 2 P. & C.R. 9, p.122.

Note 15: Insert on the last line after "comment on this": nor, on the appeal from the Court of Appeal, did the House of Lords [2004] 2 A.C. 42.

(3) *Immediate, unconditional lump sum*

(a) Lump sum

1–013   Delete "and" in the last line but three of the paragraph.

Add at the end of the paragraph: Clauses 100 and 101 of the Courts Bill have, with numbers unchanged, reached the statute book as ss.100 and 101 of the Courts Act 2003.

(b) Immediate

1–016   NOTE 44: Insert at the beginning of the note: *Firth* was followed in *Howarth v Whittaker* [2003] Lloyd's Rep. Med. 235 where it was past care costs that were in issue.

3. OBJECT OF AN AWARD OF DAMAGES

(1) *The principle of compensation*

NOTE 57: Add at the end: And see para.1–002, above.   **1–021**

(3) *Compensation greater than loss*

NOTE 2: Add at the end: *cf.*, at para.32–017A, below, *Lagden v O'Connor*   **1–027**
[2004] 1 A.C. 1067 where hiring a car from a hire car company brought additional benefits for which the claimant did not have to account: see especially Lord Hope at *ibid.*, paras 30 to 35.

BOOK ONE

PART ONE

THE HEADS OF COMPENSATORY DAMAGES

CHAPTER 2

PECUNIARY LOSSES

I. CONTRACT

1. BASIC PECUNIARY LOSSES: THE NORMAL MEASURE OF DAMAGES

(1) *The normal measure of damages*

(a) Breach by transferor

(ii) Delayed performance

NOTE 14: For para.22–005, 964 read para.22–005.   **2–008**

2. CONSEQUENTIAL PECUNIARY LOSSES

(1) *Gains prevented by the breach*

(a) Loss of use, loss of profits, interest

Insert a new note at the end of the paragraph: **2–026**

NOTE 64a: In *Earl's Terrace Properties Ltd v Nilsson Design Ltd* [2004] B.L.R. 273 this paragraph was cited (at *ibid.*, para.63) and applied. See the case at para.26–008A, below.

(b) Loss of future reputation, of publicity, of credit

2–028   NOTE 76: Insert at the end of the first sentence: but not a theatrical production company for loss of publicity through not receiving credits in programmes for a highly successful play: *Brighton v Jones* [2004] E.M.L.R. 26, p.507; see at *ibid.*, para.89 *et seq.*

NOTE 84: Insert after the reference in the note to *Johnson v Unisys Ltd*: a qualification itself qualified by *Eastwood v Magnox Electric plc* [2005] 1 A.C. 503: see para.28–019, below.

(2) *Expenses caused by the breach*

2–031   NOTE 3: Add at the end: *Contigroup Companies Inc v Glencore AG* [2005] 1 Lloyd's Rep. 241 (damages and settlement).

(3) *Expenses rendered futile by the breach: an alternative to recovery for gains prevented by the breach*

Insert new paragraphs after para.2–039:

2–039A   The claim for wasted expenditure received short shrift from the Court of Appeal in *Filobake Ltd v Rondo Ltd* [2005] EWCA Civ 563, May 11; it was there described as being based on "the *Cullinane* principle" (*ibid.*, para.60). The defendant had supplied the claimant with equipment for use in its business as a manufacturer of pastry products. Following installation and payment the claimant came to view the equipment as unable to produce pastry in accordance with its requirements and therefore as not fit for its purpose. Its claim for damages was first and foremost for loss of profits but this claim failed miserably on the altar of proof. Fearing such failure the claimant very late in the day had advanced in the alternative the claim for wasted expenditure, seeking leave to amend particulars of claim and grounds of appeal accordingly. Leave was refused. The Court of Appeal pointed out that, while a claimant may always have a choice between lost profits and wasted expenditure, it was not permissible to run the two claims in the alternative (*ibid.* para.64). Indeed since the authorities indicated that the claim for wasted expenditure was available only where it was impossible for the claimant to prove what profit had been lost, such a claim could hardly be available to a claimant who was attempting, even if unsuccessfully, to recover for loss of profits (*ibid.*, para.65). In any event, as a matter of substance the losing nature of the contract here could be shown, even with the burden of proof of this on the defendant, and claims for wasted expenditure are not available to the bad bargainer (*ibid.*, para.66). What is more difficult, however, to decide is whether the claimant should still have been entitled to recover its purchase price. The Court of Appeal, intent on refusing the amendment sought, was not prepared to go into this beyond saying that, the claimant having here lost its right to reject the equipment, it would be wrong to permit it to restore the equivalent of that right under the guise of a damages claim (*ibid.*, paras 67 and 68). Perhaps the loss of the purchase price can be considered as all part and parcel of the bad bargain. Yet in a more sympathetic context this aspect of the claim needs to be given further thought.

However, that *Cullinane* must not be carried too far is illustrated by **2–039B** *Browning v Brachers* [2005] EWCA Civ 753, June 20. The claimants ran a business of rearing goats on their farm. In their claim against the defendant for selling them a diseased goatherd (see the facts further at para.8–055C, below), *Cullinane* was invoked to argue that they could not claim both for the resultant diminution in the value of the farm and for the resultant loss of profits. The argument was rejected both at trial and by the Court of Appeal. Such a claim did not involve double counting as the claimants had two distinct assets, the business and the farm, so that a combination of compensation for the revenue loss of profits and the capital loss in the value of the farm was appropriate: *ibid.*, paras 140 and 253.

II. TORT

2. CONSEQUENTIAL PECUNIARY LOSSES

(3) *Expenses rendered futile by the tort*

NOTE 13: Add at the end: But there could be no recovery for the expense of **2–052** an operation rendered futile because it led to the death of the patient: *Batt v Highgate Private Hospital* [2005] P.I.Q.R. Q p.1. See further on this case at paras 36–018 and 36–123, below.

CHAPTER 3

NON-PECUNIARY LOSSES

I. TORT

(1) *Pain and suffering and loss of amenities*

3–006   NOTE 12: Insert before the last sentence of the note: The House of Lords' affirmation of the Court of Appeal in *Wainwright v Home Office* [2004] 2 A.C. 406 turns on there being held to be no right of action for the negligent infliction of distress short of actual recognised psychiatric illness, with opinion reserved on whether intentional infliction of such distress would give rise to liability. *Wilkinson v Downton* [1897] 2 Q.B. 57, well known for being the earliest of the successful nervous shock cases which was here very much to the fore in argument and decision, is to be understood as covering only situations of psychiatric illness.

(4) *Mental distress*

3–011   NOTE 36: Add after the reference to *Scutt v Lomax*: *Bryant v Macklin* [2005] EWCA Civ 762, June 23, and *Dennis v Ministry of Defence* [2003] 2 E.G.L.R. 121.

Insert in the text immediately after note 38: Breach of confidence, where it is breach of personal or individual confidence as distinct from breach of commercial confidence, is beginning to attract damages for injured feelings: *Campbell v MGN Ltd* [2002] E.M.L.R. 30, p.617 (damages not in issue in CA or HL); *Douglas v Hello! Ltd (No.5)* [2003] E.M.L.R. 31, p.641 (these damages not in issue in CA); also *Cornelius v de Taranto* [2001] E.M.L.R. 12, p.329 (again damages not in issue in CA) and *Archer v Williams* [2003] E.M.L.R. 38, p.869; all at para.40–025A, below.

NOTE 43: Add at the end: *British Telecommunications plc v Reid* [2004] I.R.L.R. 327, CA is a further case of racial discrimination in employment where the Court of Appeal affirmed an award of £6,000 for injury to the employee's feelings, exacerbated by the indignity of having to undergo a totally unjustified investigation resulting from the discriminatory act by way of a racially abusive remark, together with £2,000 in aggravated damages, stemming from the high-handed and insulting conduct of the employer defendant in promoting the person responsible for the racially abusive remark while the matter was still under investigation. Awards for injured feelings in discrimination cases are not subject to tax: see *Orthet Ltd v Vince-Cain* [2005] I.C.R. 374, EAT at para.14–011, n.29, below.

NOTE 44: Add at the end: In *Collins Stewart Ltd v Financial Times Ltd* [2005] EWHC 262 (QB), February 25, a defamation case, it has again been rightly held that aggravated damages were not to be awarded to a corporate claimant with no feelings to injure: *ibid.*, paras 30 and 31. Rather than saying that *Messenger* was wrong, Gray J. unconvincingly distinguished it on the ground that it concerned exemplary damages: *ibid.*, para.32.

II. CONTRACT

(3) *Mental distress*

NOTE 87: Add: "In proceedings which have cast a long shadow over the common law": *per* Lord Nicholls in *Eastwood v Magnox Electric plc* [2005] 1 A.C. 503, para.1.   **3–019**

Add a new note at the end of the paragraph: **3–024**

NOTE 29a: Disappointment at not receiving publicity by way of credits in programmes for a highly successful play did not sound in damages: *Brighton v Jones* [2004] E.M.L.R. 26, p.507; see at paras 87 and 88.

Add at the end of the paragraph: Lord Hoffmann's dictum in *Johnson v Unisys Ltd* was not applied in *Dunnachie v Kingston upon Hull City Council* [2005] 1 A.C. 226 but this was only in the context of unfair dismissal. The House of Lords there held that the word "loss" in the unfair dismissal legislation, specifically in s.123(1) of the Employment Rights Act 1996, did not on its true construction include non-pecuniary loss, so that an employee could not recover under the section compensation for loss arising from the manner of his dismissal, including humiliation, injury to feelings and distress. Nothing further on mental distress and non-financial loss appears in the House of Lords in *Eastwood v Magnox Electric plc* [2005] 1 A.C. 503: see the case at para.28–019, below.   **3–029**

Add a new note at the end of the paragraph: **3–030**

NOTE 59a: But will remain the position for unfair dismissal: *Dunnachie v Kingston upon Hull City Council* [2005] 1 A.C. 226 at para.3–029, above.

(4) *Social discredit*

3–031   NOTE 69: Add: But Lord Hoffmann's comments have not been applied to
unfair dismissal: *Dunnachie v Kingston upon Hull City Council* [2005] 1 A.C.
226 at para.3–029, above.

BOOK ONE

PART TWO

THE LIMITS OF COMPENSATORY DAMAGES

CHAPTER 4

THE GENERAL PROBLEM OF LIMITS

1. INTERRELATION OF EXISTENCE AND EXTENT OF LIABILITY

(1) *Duty, scope of duty and remoteness*

Insert a new note after the penultimate sentence of the paragraph: **4-004**

NOTE 19a: No duty of care is owed to a local authority which would allow it to recover its costs of caring for the victim of a tortious injury from the tortfeasor: *London Borough of Islington v University College London Hospital NHS Trust* [2005] EWCA Civ 596, June 16 (at para.35–209A, below).

NOTE 26: Add at the end: Recovery from the employer for psychiatric ill- **4-005** ness arising from stress at work was denied in *Pratley v Surrey CC* [2004] P.I.Q.R. P p.252, CA because not reasonably foreseeable, being an issue of remoteness rather than duty.

2. INTERRELATION OF VARIOUS FACETS OF THE EXTENT OF LIABILITY

(1) *Contributory negligence, and remoteness and mitigation*

Add at the end of the paragraph: *Barings plc v Coopers & Lybrand* [2003] **4-018** Lloyd's Rep. I.R. 566, an extremely lengthy litigation arising out of the disastrous Barings collapse, provides an interesting and unusual application, to events following upon the wrong, of contributory negligence and remoteness in combination. The defendant auditors had negligently failed to uncover unauthorised trading by an employee which had resulted over time in huge losses to the claimant employer companies, but mismanagement of the companies was such that for long the unauthorised trading, and hence the losses, went undetected by them. The trial judge after a very lengthy and thorough analysis (*ibid.*, paras 893 to 910, paras 945 to 964 and paras 1058 to 1068) concluded that there had been increasing contributory negligence, starting at 50 and finishing at 80 per cent, until eventually the chain of causation had been broken (*ibid.*, para.1069). Thus for a time only contributory negligence was in issue; then remoteness took over (see *ibid.*, para.892).

4–019   NOTE 76: Add at the end: The rule in *The Liesbosch* has at last been abandoned in *Lagden v O'Connor* [2004] 1 A.C. 1067: see para.6–101A, below.

NOTE 77: Add at the end: Lord Collins's dictum has rightly been said to be difficult to reconcile with the rule in *The Liesbosch* [1933] A.C. 449, making a distinction without a difference: see *Lagden v O'Connor* [2004] 1 A.C. 1067 at para.51, *per* Lord Hope.

4–021   Insert a new note after the first sentence of the paragraph:

NOTE 87a: *Barings plc v Coopers & Lybrand* [2003] Lloyd's Rep. I.R. 566 gave rise to issues not only of contributory negligence and remoteness (see the case at para.4–018, above) but also of mitigation (see the case at paras 7–123A to 7–123D, below).

(3) *Remoteness and certainty*

4–024   NOTE 1: Add: While there is no difficulty in distinguishing the one from the other there may be an interaction between certainty and contributory negligence which requires to be resolved with care. This was so in *Sharpe v Addison* [2004] P.N.L.R. 23, p.426, CA: see para.8–058, below.

CHAPTER 5

REDUCTION OF DAMAGES FOR CONTRIBUTORY NEGLIGENCE

NOTE 2: Add at the end: Similarly in *Sowden v Lodge* [2005] 1 W.L.R. 2129,   **5–002**
CA where, in deciding whether the claimant's accommodation and care
should be by a private arrangement or a residential arrangement (facts at
para.35–159B, below), the Court of Appeal rightly held that it should not
take into account that the claimant might be unable to afford a private
arrangement for life because, on account of her contributory negligence, she
would recover only half of the damages for full liability. The damages were
to be assessed applying ordinary principles and it was the sum so assessed
which was to be reduced for contributory negligence. The wording of both
s.1(1) and s.1(2) clearly pointed in this direction. See *ibid.*, paras 74 to 84
(nothing in the headnote on this issue).

1. LIABILITY IN TORT

(2) *Apportionment*

NOTE 16: Add at the end: In *Sahib Foods Ltd v Paskin Kyriakides Sands*   **5–007**
[2004] P.N.L.R. 22, p.403, where questions arose of how far the causing and
the spreading of a fire was the fault of the defendant and how far the fault of
the claimant, causation and blameworthiness, and even duty, required
lengthy analysis by the Court of Appeal. For an unusual aspect of causation
and blame see *Barker v Saint Gobain Pipelines plc* [2004] P.I.Q.R. P p.579, CA
at para.6–017, below.

2. LIABILITY IN CONTRACT

(2) *Apportionment*

NOTE 61: Add at the end: *Barings plc v Coopers & Lybrand* [2003] Lloyd's   **5–016**
Rep. I.R. 566: 50 per cent escalating to 60 per cent and then to 80 per cent
(see the case at para.4–018, above); *Slattery v Moore Stephens* [2004] P.N.L.R.

14, p.241: 50 per cent reduction (on part of the damages; claim by client of accountant).

3. LIABILITY UNDER THE MISREPRESENTATION ACT

5–017   NOTE 65: Add at the end: The reason that no deduction was made in *Gran Gelato* is that one induced to act upon a representation should be entitled to rely upon its truth without the representor, who intended the representee to act on it, being able to say that its correctness could have been checked by him. This may explain the enigmatic statement of the trial judge in *Peekay Intermark Ltd v Australian and New Zealand Banking Group Ltd* [2005] EWHC 830 (Comm), May 25, at para.98, where damages were awarded under s.2(1) of the 1967 Act (see the case at para.41–049, below), that in the absence of a plea of contributory negligence he did not have to consider whether contributory negligence would in principle be applicable to the case in the light of *Gran Gelato*.

CHAPTER 6

REMOTENESS OF DAMAGE

I. TORT

(A) CAUSATION

1. CAUSE IN FACT AND CAUSE IN LAW

(2) *Cause in law*

(b) Legal causation and *The Wagon Mound*

Insert a new paragraph after para.6–012:

[21]

6–012A   The boundary between causation and foreseeability has been interestingly illustrated by *Essa v Laing Ltd* [2004] I.C.R. 746, CA. The Court of Appeal there held, by a majority, that in the case before it, a statutory tort claim under the Race Relations Act 1976, the test for recoverable loss was causation without the superimposition of a test of reasonable foreseeability. A racial taunt by his foreman at work caused the claimant immense distress which led to his leaving his job and to severe depression amounting to psychiatric illness. The defendant employers' argument, which had been accepted by the employment tribunal, that they were not liable for the illness because only the distress was foreseeable was rejected on two separate grounds. The first ground for rejection — the second is dealt with at para.6–091A, below — was that, in the circumstances of direct discrimination by racial abuse in the face of the victim, the victim should be compensated for loss which arises naturally and directly from the wrong, whether or not that loss was foreseeable: see Pill L.J. at *ibid.*, para.39. Clarke L.J., agreeing, examined the policy behind the statute and concluded that, since it had been introduced to remedy a very great evil, it should be sufficient for the claimant to show that his injury was caused by the act of discrimination (*ibid.*, para.49). Pill L.J., pointing out that the facts of the case were akin to the torts of assault and battery — where it is known that reasonable foreseeability is not a requirement — in that there was deliberate conduct towards and in the presence of the victim though the abuse was verbal and not physical, added that the position might be otherwise where the discrimination took other forms (*ibid.*, para.39). "Different considerations may apply within the confines of a single tort": *ibid.*, para.34. In so saying he was adverting to Lord Nicholls's analysis in *Kuwait Airways Corp v Iraqi Airways Co* [2002] 2 A.C. 883, which was given detailed consideration in all three judgments, where in the context of conversion Lord Nicholls drew a distinction in relation to conversion between the converter who was dishonest and the converter who was not (see para.33–066 of the main text). Rix L.J., dissenting, wished to retain here the requirement of reasonable foreseeability. He could find nothing in the statute which required a conclusion that the rule of remoteness for this statutory tort should be one of pure causation (*ibid.*, para.105) and he expressed himself as reluctant to promote a test which varied with the nature of the discrimination (*ibid.*, para.106).

2. CAUSE IN FACT: THE NORM AND THE EXCEPTIONS

(1) *The norm*

6–014   NOTE 30: Add: Similar is *Ward v The Leeds Teaching Hospitals NHS Trust* [2004] Lloyd's Rep. Med. 530 where a mother's psychiatric illness was caused by the death of her child and not by events surrounding the death: see *ibid.* paras 23 and 24. See too *John Mowlem Construction plc v Neil F. Jones & Co* [2004] P.N.L.R. 45, p.925, CA: causation negatived where solicitor's advice to notify insurers of a potential claim would have been ignored had it been given.

NOTE 31: Add at the end: or simply that the person's injured condition would have been the same without the defendant's intervention: *Steel v Joy* [2004] 1 W.L.R. 3002, CA at para.6–021A, below.

(2) *The exceptions*

(a) Negligence

Add at the end of the paragraph: The Court of Appeal has taken *Fairchild* **6–017** further in *Barker v Saint Gobain Pipelines plc* [2004] P.I.Q.R. P p.579, CA by holding in favour of the claimant whose husband had died from mesothelioma, having been exposed to asbestos not only when working for the defendant but when self-employed. Keene L.J. said that "it is not a condition of liability under the principle in *Fairchild* that the injury must have been caused by someone's tortious act, so long as it is established that the defendant in breach of its duty to the [deceased] exposed him to the risk of contracting mesothelioma and that risk eventuated": *ibid.*, para.50. It was accepted however that there should be a reduction in the damages for contributory negligence. The case may go to the Lords.

NOTE 45: Add at the end: The material contribution approach based on **6–019** *McGhee* and *Fairchild* does not appear to have been pursued by the claimant in the Lords in *Gregg v Scott* [2005] 2 A.C. 176: see the case at paras 8–032A to 8–032D, below.

NOTE 48: Add: Nothing said at this point in *Hatton* is affected by *Barber v Somerset CC* [2004] 1 W.L.R. 1089, HL where the House of Lords allowed the further appeal of one of the appellants in four conjoined appeals which had been heard earlier in the Court of Appeal under the title *Hatton v Sutherland*.

Insert a new paragraph after para.6–021:

Two consecutive injuries also fell to be considered in *Steel v Joy* [2004] 1 **6–021A** W.L.R. 3002, CA. The claimant was the victim of an accident involving the first defendant and later of another involving the second. The symptoms of his congenital spinal condition were accelerated by a good number of years by the first accident; the second accident would have had the same effect as the first if the first had not already occurred. The Court of Appeal held the second defendant not responsible for the consequences of the first injury even though but for the first accident the second one would have caused similar injury. Since the claimant had already suffered the damage at the hands of the first defendant, the second defendant had not caused it. Neither *Rahman* nor *Baker* was said to be in point. Instead, *Performance Cars v Abraham* [1962] 1 Q.B. 33, CA, a similar case but in a different context (see it at para.32–010 of the main text), was followed. *Steel* is reported together with a prior case,

Halsey, primarily on an issue of costs; the causation issue, arising only in *Steel*, is at paras 55 to 70.

Insert new paragraphs after para.6–023:

6–023A   The House of Lords has indeed affirmed the Court of Appeal, though only by a bare majority: *Chester v Afshar* [2005] 1 A.C. 134. The majority accepted that the defendant's failure to warn neither affected the risk nor was the effective cause of the injury so that the claimant could not satisfy the conventional tests of causation. However, the majority further considered that the issue of causation was to be addressed by reference to the scope of the doctor's duty to advise his patients of the risks of treatment, a duty which was closely connected with the need for the patient's consent and was central to her right to make an informed choice. In the light of these considerations justice required a narrow modification of traditional causation principles to vindicate the claimant's right of choice and to provide a remedy for the breach. Thus the majority was prepared to make a further limited modification — the first was in *Fairchild* (see paras 6–018 and 6–019 of the main text) — of conventional causation principles.

6–023B   It is thought that this controversial decision has a very limited application and is unlikely to step outside its own context, the context of the duty to warn of the dangers and risks of medical treatment. The correlative right of the patient is one of great significance, the duty in the absence of imposing liability is deprived of its force and emptied of its content, and it is difficult to think of other rights and duties which adhere to a similar pattern. Of course the decision was bound to encourage claimants to try to have it applied to professional negligence, other than clinical negligence, where very commonly there is a failure to warn or to advise. Such attempts however have been rapidly struck down by the Court of Appeal on two occasions, in *White v Paul Davidson & Taylor* [2005] P.N.L.R. 15, p.245, CA where a solicitor had failed to advise his client that the effect of a notice to quit was to terminate a tenancy, which failure deprived the client of the opportunity to decide whether or not to take the course of resisting possession proceedings even to appeal, and again in *Beary v Pall Mall Investments* [2005] EWCA 415, April 19, where a financial adviser had failed to advise his client that a risk-free annuity would have been an alternative investment to the high-risk one that he was proposing.

3. CAUSE IN LAW: DIRECT CONSEQUENCES

6–028   NOTE 86: Add at the end: But see now para.6–101A, below for the abandonment of *The Liesbosch* [1933] A.C. 449 in *Lagden v O'Connor* [2004] 1 A.C. 1067.

4. CAUSE IN LAW: CONSEQUENCES FOLLOWING UPON A NEW INTERVENING FORCE

(1) *Intervening acts of a third party*

(b) Acts where the third party is a free chooser

Insert a new note at the end of the paragraph: 6–039

NOTE 40a: For the resolution (moot on account of no liability) of a somewhat unusual question of remoteness involving third party acts in the area of economic torts see *Douglas v Hello! Ltd (No.8)* [2005] EWCA Civ 595, May 18, at paras 238 to 242.

(ii) Wrongful acts

Insert a new note at the end of the paragraph: 6–052

NOTE 14a: *cf.* the same result in *Hamilton-Jones v David & Snape* [2004] 1 W.L.R. 924 at para.6–131, below. The facts were "strikingly similar" (*per* Neuberger J. at *ibid.*, para.64) but the claim was in contract.

(2) *Intervening acts of the claimant*

(a) Acts where the claimant is not a completely free chooser

(i) Acts by claimants not fully responsible: adults and children

Insert a new note at the end of the paragraph: 6–060

NOTE 65a: In *Gough v Upshire Primary School* [2002] E.L.R. 169 the judge was prepared to say that an eight-year-old playing on a swing could be held contributorily negligent to a substantial degree: see *ibid.*, para.25.

(ii) Acts by claimants safeguarding their own interests

NOTE 87: Add at the end: *The Metagama*, and other shipping cases at 6–063 para.6–071 of the main text, were referred to the court in *Morris v Richards* [2004] P.I.Q.R. Q p.30, CA in the context of holding that a physically injured claimant taking new employment and then losing it was not thereby disqualified from recovering damages for loss of earnings in respect of the period following the loss of her new position.

(b) Acts where the claimant is a free chooser

Insert a new note after the second sentence of the paragraph: 6–069

NOTE 23a: In *Barings plc v Coopers & Lybrand* [2003] Lloyd's Rep. I.R. 566 where the claimants, three companies in the Barings group which collapsed on account of the unauthorised trading of a fraudulent employee, sued their auditor for negligence in its audit, leading to a failure to uncover the unauthorised trading and to consequent mounting losses, there was explored in massive detail (*ibid.*, paras 781 to 879) whether the acts and omissions of the claimants in serious mismanagement broke the chain of causation and, if so, at what point in time.

6–070 NOTE 27: Add at the end: See too *Barings plc v Coopers & Lybrand* [2003] Lloyd's Rep. I.R. 566 at para.4–018, above; the case was contract (at para.6–139, below) but the decision would have been the same in tort.

6–071 Insert after the second sentence of the paragraph: The claimant and the defendant in *Arkin v Borchard Lines Ltd* [2003] 2 Lloyd's Rep. 225 were fierce competitors in the provision of liner operating services. The claimant, suing for heavy trading losses it had suffered in consequence of the defendant's breach of the Treaty of Rome, had continued in the market, in which the defendant had achieved a dominant position, and as a result had incurred these losses. Since it was held that no reasonable liner operator would have remained in the market, the decision to remain and the decision to reduce rates to suicide levels were so irrational that they could not be justified, and therefore the predominant cause of the claimant's continuing losses was held to be its failure to withdraw from the market.

(B) SCOPE OF PROTECTION: THE LIMITS OF POLICY

2. FORESEEABLE DAMAGE CAUSED IN AN UNFORESEEABLE MANNER OR TO AN UNFORESEEABLE DEGREE WHERE A BREACH OF DUTY TO THE CLAIMANT TO TAKE CARE HAS BEEN ESTABLISHED

(1) *Direct consequences*

(a) Existing states of affairs: physical abnormalities of the claimant or of his property

6–090 NOTE 37: Add at the end: Claims for damages under s.76 of the Civil Aviation Act 1982 attract the normal common law rules with their distinction between primary and secondary victims: *Glen v Korean Airlines Co Ltd* [2003] Q.B. 1386.

NOTE 39: Add: In *British Steel plc v Simmons* [2004] P.I.Q.R. P p.33, HL where there was immediate physical injury, recovery was allowed for subsequent psychiatric injury which, it was alleged, sprang not from the accident itself but from the claimant's anger at the happening of the accident. Not only was there no reason to draw a distinction on this basis but it was doubted if such a distinction could be realistically drawn at all.

NOTE 43: Add at the end: Psychiatric illness arising from stress at work does not lead to liability on the employer where held to be not reasonably foreseeable as in *Pratley v Surrey CC* [2004] P.I.Q.R. P p.252, CA.

Insert a new note at the end of the paragraph: 6–091

NOTE 49a: *Page v Smith* was applied by the House of Lords in a Scots appeal to a rather difficult situation so as to allow recovery for an employee's psychiatric illness in *Simmons v British Steel plc* [2004] I.C.R. 585, HL. See the valuable analysis of the authorities by Lord Rodger at *ibid.*, paras 53 to 67. And for another interesting application of *Page v Smith*, here by the Court of Appeal, see *Donachie v Chief Constable of Greater Manchester* [2004] EWCA Civ 405, April 7.

Insert a new paragraph after paragraph 6–091:

Somewhat similar is *Essa v Laing Ltd* [2004] I.C.R. 746, CA, where injury   6–091A
to feelings arising from racial abuse was reasonably foreseeable but psychiatric illness, which occurred, was not. There were two grounds on which the decision for the claimant in this case was based — the first ground concerned causation and foreseeability and is at para.6–012A, above, where the facts will also be found — and the second ground upon which it was held, by a majority and by the same majority as with the first, that the lack of reasonable foreseeability did not matter was that the two injuries were of the same type and not of a different kind. Praying in aid the reasoning of the House of Lords in *Page v Smith* [1996] A.C. 155 (at para.6–090 of the main text) that physical injury and psychiatric injury are of the same type, Clarke L.J. said that he did not see why injury to feelings and psychiatric injury should not also be so treated (at [2004] I.R.C. 746, CA, para.55); indeed he said that in his opinion it would be very odd, in the light of *Page*, if foreseeabiliy of injury to feelings were not sufficient to obviate the need to show foreseeability of psychiatric injury (at *ibid.*, para.65). Pill L.J. pointed out that injury to feelings and psychiatric injury can show a substantial degree of overlap and that this did not support a conclusion that the injuries are of a different kind (at *ibid.*, para.42). For the dissenting Rix L.J., on the other hand, they were indeed of a different kind, injury to feelings being a common-day experience and something distinct from illness (at *ibid.*, para.117).

(b) Existing states of affairs: pecuniary abnormalities of the claimant or of his property

(i) Strength

6–098   Add at the end of the paragraph: In *Sandeman Coprimar SA v Transitos y Transportes Integrales SL* [2003] Q.B. 1270, CA the Court of Appeal undoubtedly accepted that in a negligent conversion the test was reasonable foreseeability: see *ibid.*, paras 25 to 31. The case is considered at paras 6–184A and 6–184B, below.

(ii) Weakness

Insert a new paragraph after para.6–101:

6–101A   After being distinguished nearly out of existence *The Liesbosch* [1933] A.C. 449 has, in this aspect, been finally put to rest by the House of Lords in *Lagden v O'Connor* [2004] 1 A.C. 1067 where an impecunious claimant was held entitled to recover hire car company charges that a claimant who was not impecunious could not have recovered. While only a majority favoured allowing the claimant recovery on account of impecuniosity in the particular circumstances — the facts of *Lagden* are at para.32–017A, below — the House was unanimous that the time had come to bury the rule in *The Liesbosch*. Lord Hope, after reviewing the authorities nearly all of which are dealt with at para.6–101 of the main text, said at [2004] 1 A.C. 1067, para.61:

> "It is not necessary for us to say that *The Liesbosch* was wrongly decided. But it is clear that the law has moved on, and that the correct test of remoteness today is whether the loss was reasonably foreseeable. The wrongdoer must take his victim as he finds him: talem qualem, as Lord Collins said in the *Clippens Oil* case [1907] A.C. 291, 303. This rule applies to the economic state of the victim in the same way as it applies to his physical and mental vulnerability."

And he ended his speech, *ibid.*, para.62, with: "I would hold that this rule [in *The Liesbosch*] should now be departed from".

(c) Other existing states of affairs

6–106   NOTE 55: Add at the end: And in *Sandeman Coprimar SA v Transitos y Transportes Integrales SL* [2003] Q.B. 1270, CA it was held that loss through payment of duty on importation of goods was not of the same type as loss through payment on a guarantee in respect of such duty and that therefore liability could not be imposed: see *ibid.*, paras 28 and 39. The case, dealt with at paras 6–184A and 6–184B, below, was in negligence as well as conversion.

3. DAMAGE TO A SECONDARY INTEREST WHERE A SEPARATE LIABILITY IN RESPECT OF A PRIMARY INTEREST HAS BEEN ESTABLISHED

NOTE 34: Add at the end: But the rule in *The Liesbosch* [1933] A.C. 449 has **6–119** at last been abandoned in *Lagden v O'Connor* [2004] 1 A.C. 1067: see para.6–101A, above.

4. DAMAGE OUTSIDE THE SCOPE OF THE DUTY

NOTE 53: Add: The decision of Langley J. has been reversed: [2003] **6–124** 2 B.C.L.C. 603, CA; see the Court of Appeal's discussion of scope of duty and causation (together with loss of a chance) at *ibid.*, paras 78 *et seq.*

NOTE 54: Add at the end: There are however cases in which cause necessarily predominates over scope of duty, as appears to have been so on one of the issues in *Green v Alexander Johnson* [2005] EWCA Civ 775, June 28, an appeal on the computation of damages arising out of a barrister's negligence: see the discussion at *ibid.*, para.23 *et seq.*

II. CONTRACT

(A) CAUSATION

2. CONSEQUENCES FOLLOWING UPON A NEW INTERVENING FORCE

(1) *Intervening acts of a third party*

Add at the end of the paragraph: Another case is *Hamilton-Jones v David* **6–131** *& Snape* [2004] 1 W.L.R. 924 where the negligence of the claimant's solicitor gave the opportunity to the Tunisian father of her children to remove them out of the country to Tunisia.

(2) *Intervening acts of the claimant*

Add at the end of the paragraph: *Barings plc v Coopers & Lybrand* [2003] **6–139** Lloyd's Rep. I.R. 566 presents an intermediate situation where the negligent failure in detection of the defendant auditors was held to be causative for a time and then to cease to be causative. The case, the facts of which are at para.4–018, above, is one of intervening omissions rather than intervening acts of the claimant.

(B) SCOPE OF PROTECTION: CONTEMPLATION OF THE PARTIES

4. THE DEGREE OF LIKELIHOOD REQUIRED

Insert a new paragraph after para.6–155:

6–155A   A further case, and at House of Lords level, allowing recovery for damage held not too remote is *Jackson v Royal Bank of Scotland* [2005] 1 W.L.R. 377, HL. The defendant bank had negligently sent not to the claimants, who were importers of goods for sale to customers, but to the claimants' principal customer documents which revealed the claimants' substantial profit margin on their sales to the customer causing the customer in future to buy direct from the claimants' supplier. The House of Lords rejected, as had the courts below, the defendant bank's argument that it could not have contemplated or foreseen that its disclosure would lead to the termination of the claimants' trading relationship with their customer so that the claimants' loss of profits consequent on the termination was too remote: see *ibid.*, paras 27 to 29. At the same time the House of Lords held that the Court of Appeal had gone wrong in limiting the bank's liability for loss of these profits to a period of one year from termination on the ground of remoteness. By limiting the recovery to one year's loss of profits the Court of Appeal would appear, said Lord Hope giving the leading speech, to have "misunderstood the effect of the rules that were identified in *Hadley v Baxendale*": *ibid.*, para.25. Accordingly, the House restored the judge's award of lost profits over a number of years, though on a decreasing basis as the likelihood that the customer would in any event have terminated the trading relationship increased, going only to the time when an award for a further year would have been too speculative. See on all this *ibid.*, paras 35 to 38.

5. THE DEGREE OF KNOWLEDGE REQUIRED

(1) *Actual and imputed knowledge*

6–165   Add at the end of the paragraph: And the common ground between the two rules, or the two limbs of the rule, in *Hadley v Baxendale* is again emphasised by the House of Lords in *Jackson v Royal Bank of Scotland* [2005] 1 W.L.R. 377, HL (facts at para.6–155A, above): see in particular the speech of Lord Walker at paras 46 to 49.

6–166   Add at the end of the paragraph: And *Louis Dreyfus Trading Ltd v Reliance Trading Ltd* [2004] 2 Lloyd's Rep. 243, illustrates precisely the operation of Devlin J.'s statement (in the main text in this paragraph) that damages must be assessed by reference to a sub-sale in the contemplation of the parties even if this does not suit the claimant. Since the parties to the sale of a cargo of sugar had in their contemplation a sub-sale by the buyer already made and on which the buyer might eventually have made a profit, the sub-sale, it was held, could be brought into account against the buyer. However, it was for the defendant seller to demonstrate on the evidence that the impact of the sub-sale was such that the *prima facie* measure of damages was inappropriate, and the matter was sent back to the arbitral tribunal initially deciding the case to give the defendant a chance to prove this, the arbitrators having applied the *prima facie* measure without considering the possibility that it might be displaced. See the case further at para.20–100, below.

(2) *Extent to which knowledge will be imputed*

Insert a new note after the colon on the penultimate line of the paragraph: **6–167**

NOTE 59a: For a somewhat unusual illustration of this, see the contractual aspects of *Sandeman Coprimar SA v Transitos y Transportes Integrales SL* [2003] Q.B. 1270, CA at paras 6–184A and 6–184B, below.

(3) *Effect of actual knowledge*

Insert a new note at the end of the paragraph: **6–174**

NOTE 84a: In *Jackson v Royal Bank of Scotland plc* [2005] 1 W.L.R. 377, HL (facts at para.6–155A, above) the House of Lords corrected the Court of Appeal's "error of principle" (*ibid.*, para.36) and confirmed that the time for assessing what is within the parties' reasonable contemplation — to which their knowledge would be relevant — is the time of the making of the contract and not, as the Court of Appeal had held, the time of its breach. Lord Hope, making the leading speech, pointed out that this clear rule gave the parties the opportunity to limit their liability in damages when they are making their contract: see *ibid.*, paras 35 and 36. For what precisely must be in the contemplation of the parties at the time of contracting see the interesting points made in *Bluestorm Ltd v Portvale Holdings Ltd* [2004] H.L.R. 49, p.939, CA at *ibid.*, paras 28 and 29.

NOTE 2: Add at the end: *Mulvenna v Royal Bank of Scotland plc* [2003] **6–177** EWCA Civ 1112, July 25, is a case where, in holding against the claimant, the court relied on the need to show that the defendant accepted the risk to which the special circumstances gave rise: see especially at *ibid.*, para.26.

NOTE 7: Add at the end: Compare the possibility of taking irrecoverable losses into account to support a claim for specific relief, at para.13–016, below.

7. MAIN TYPES OF CONTRACT IN WHICH THE RULE IN *HADLEY V BAXENDALE* HAS BEEN DEVELOPED

(1) *Breach of contract by seller of goods*

6–182   NOTE 31: Insert after the reference to *Elbinger Aktiengesellschaft v Armstrong*: and *Contigroup Companies Inc v Glencore AG* [2005] 1 Lloyd's Rep. 241.

(2) *Breach of contract by carrier of goods*

Insert new paragraphs after para.6–184:

6–184A   An interesting and complex case involving carriage of goods is *Sandeman Coprimar SA v Transitos y Transportes Integrales SL* [2003] Q.B. 1270, CA. The claimants were exporters of whisky to Spain. From the Spanish tax authorities they acquired tax seals of nominal value for use in sealing their whisky bottles to indicate that Spanish excise duty had been duly paid by them. They contracted with the first defendant for the carriage by road from Spain to Scotland of cartons containing these tax seals. The first defendant sub-contracted the carriage to the second defendant who in turn sub-contracted it to the third defendant. The cargo was lost in the course of carriage and the claimants were required to pay to the Spanish tax authorities under a guarantee of which the defendants had no specific knowledge an amount equivalent to the excise duty which would have been recovered on the bottles to which the seals should have been attached. The claimants claimed this amount from the defendants by way of common law damages — there were also complex claims under the Convention scheduled to the Carriage of Goods by Road Act 1965 not relevant here — and the judge below held against the first defendant as it was aware of the nature of the seals and the consequences that would attend their loss, and for the second and third defendants as neither could reasonably have appreciated the nature of the goods in the cartons or the consequences of their loss (see at *ibid.*, para.21).

6–184B   Whether the Court of Appeal would have upheld the judge's decision against the first defendant in what was a clear contractual claim cannot be known since the first defendant had become insolvent and took no part in the appeal hearing. The Court of Appeal had however no difficulty in affirming the judge's decision for the second and third defendants. While recognising that "there can be problems in applying a test of foreseeability to carriers who handle consolidated containers of many different varieties of goods", Lord Phillips delivering the judgment of the court concluded that:

> "no carrier without specific knowledge of the nature of [tax seals] and of the guarantee that has to be given to the Spanish authorities for their release, could envisage that the loss of a number of cartons could give

rise to the type of liability experienced by [the claimants] in this case":
ibid., para.28.

In this however the court was taking the view that the second and third defendants could not be liable at common law in negligence or in conversion (see *ibid.*, para.31) since both were immune from contractual liability because as sub-bailees there was no privity of contract between them and the claimants. Yet there seems little doubt that, had privity of contract existed thereby allowing the claimants to claim in contract, the result would have been the same.

CHAPTER 7

MITIGATION OF DAMAGE

II. THE RULE AS TO AVOIDABLE LOSS: NO RECOVERY FOR LOSS WHICH THE CLAIMANT OUGHT TO HAVE AVOIDED

1. VARIOUS ASPECTS OF THE RULE

(g) Whether need to mitigate by discontinuing contractual performance

7–029   NOTE 99: Add: The issue of whether owners were bound to accept repudiation by charterers and sue for damages did make an appearance in *Ocean Marine Navigation Ltd v Koch Carbon Inc (The Dynamic)* [2003] 2 Lloyd's Rep. 693. Since it was unclear whether the arbitrator had correctly applied the relevant principles, the matter was remitted in order to examine this: see *ibid.*, paras 19 to 26.

3. ILLUSTRATIONS OF CIRCUMSTANCES RAISING THE ISSUE OF WHETHER LOSS SHOULD HAVE BEEN AVOIDED

(1) *Contract*

(a) In general: where the door to mitigation is not opened by the party in breach

(i) Sale of goods

Add at the end of the paragraph: By contrast, in *Browning v Brachers*   **7–042**
[2005] EWCA Civ 753, June 20, the Court of Appeal took the view, contrary
to that of the trial judge, that the claimants, who were complaining that the
defendant had sold them an infected goatherd (see the facts at para.8–055C,
below), were not required, in mitigation, to have taken particular steps suggested by experts in the case to control the infection: see *ibid.*, paras 138, 162
et seq. and 228 to 236.

(ii) Lease of land

Add at the end of the paragraph: Similar is *Shine v English Churches*   **7–043**
Housing Group [2004] H.LR. 42, p.727, CA where the lessee, even under a
series of court orders, for long refused to vacate the premises, making it
impossible for the lessor to effect the repairs until the lessee's eventual vaca-
tion, with the result that they took a good deal longer than they otherwise
would have done. The Court of Appeal reduced the award because the lessee's
conduct was held to constitute a failure to mitigate: see *ibid.*, paras 111 to
113.

(2) *Tort*

(i) Personal injury

Insert a new note after the heading to the paragraph: **7–056**

NOTE 9a: The commonest mitigating step for a claimant whose injuries prevent him from continuing in his former job is of course to seek such other
employment of which he is capable. Loss of a new job however will not necessarily be regarded as a failure to mitigate: see *Morris v Richards* [2004]
P.I.Q.R. Q p.30, CA at para.6–063, n.87, above.

NOTE 16: Add at the end: Nor is a personally injured claimant required to
mitigate by using a mobility allowance to obtain less costly transport under
a motability scheme: *Eagle v Chambers (No.2)* [2004] 1 W.L.R. 3081, CA at
para.35–198, below.

7–057   NOTE 18: Add at the end: In *Butler v Thompson* [2005] EWCA Civ 864, July 13, the claimant was held not to be making the most of her reduced earning capacity; she could, and should, do somewhat more.

(ii) Goods: damage and destruction

7–059   NOTE 24: For para.32–004 read para.32–005.

7–060   Add at the end of the paragraph: *Dimond v Lovell* [2002] 1 A.C. 384 was distinguished in *Lagden v O'Connor* [2004] 1 A.C. 1067 where recovery of the higher charges was allowed, the claimant being impecunious: see the case at para.32–017A, below.

4. STANDARD OF CONDUCT WHICH THE CLAIMANT MUST ATTAIN WHEN
ASSESSING WHAT STEPS SHOULD HAVE BEEN TAKEN BY HIM

(1) *The criterion of reasonableness and the standard of reasonableness*

7–066   NOTE 48: For para.32–004 read para.32–005.

Add at the end of the paragraph: *Dimond v Lovell* [2002] 1 A.C. 384 was distinguished in *Lagden v O'Connor* [2004] 1 A.C. 1067 where recovery of the higher charges was allowed, the claimant being impecunious: see the case at para.32–017A, below.

(2) *Illustrative decisions*

(b) Illustrations of what is not required of the claimant in mitigation

(iv) A claimant need not take the risk of starting an uncertain litigation against a third party

7–076   Add at the end of the paragraph: The buyer of a farm was held not to have failed to mitigate in *Williams v Glyn Owen & Co* [2004] P.N.L.R. 20, p.367, CA (facts at para.8–041, below) by not bringing an action against his vendor before bringing his action against his negligent solicitor. It was said by Jonathan Parker L.J., at *ibid.*, para.69, that it could not be assumed that a claim for damages against the vendor would have been a straightforward affair but in what way it would not have been straightforward is not revealed.

(ix) A claimant will not be prejudiced by his financial inability to take steps in mitigation

7–082   Add at the end of the paragraph: And the point at which *Clippens* takes over from *The Liesbosch* need no longer be investigated as the House of Lords has departed from the latter: see para.6–101A, above.

III. THE COROLLARY: RECOVERY FOR LOSS INCURRED IN ATTEMPTS TO MITIGATE THE DAMAGE

Add at the end of the paragraph: But the claimant in *Riyad Bank v Ahli* **7–088**
United Bank (UK) plc [2005] EWHC 279 (Comm), March 1, was held not to
have shown that it was reasonable to incur the expenses of buying out share-
holders, which increased the loss, so that the claim for such expenses could
not have succeeded: see *ibid.*, paras 168 to 172.

IV. THE RULE AS TO AVOIDED LOSS: NO RECOVERY FOR LOSS WHICH THE CLAIMANT HAS AVOIDED, UNLESS THE MATTER IS COLLATERAL

2. VARIOUS ASPECTS OF THE RULE

(c) The preliminary issue of mitigation of loss or no loss

Add at the end of the paragraph: *McKinnon v e.surv Ltd* [2003] 2 E.G.L.R. **7–097**
57 can be explained along similar lines. The property, purchased by the
claimant on the strength of the defendant's negligent report, which had been
subject to movement was so no longer and had not been since the time of the
purchase; however it would not have been possible to establish this until after
the date of purchase. In these circumstances the claimant was held entitled in
damages to the purchase price of £185,000 less the value of £148,000 not subject to movement and not to the purchase price less the value of £92,000 if
subject to that movement. The fact that £185,000 was over the true value of
£148,000 was due to the claimant having paid too high a price for the property or to defects, other than a tendency to movement, negligently undiscov-
ered by the defendant. For the result in the case to be right it must have been
the latter; if the former, the claimant should have been entitled to no damages
at all.

3. ACTIONS TAKEN AFTER THE WRONG BY THE CLAIMANT

(1) *Situations where the benefit is generally taken into account*

(a) Sale

Substitute for the first two lines of the paragraph: The converse situation, **7–103**
where the breach of contract was not by the seller and supplier of the goods
but by the buyer to whom they were supplied, arose in *Hill v Showell*.

(b) Other situations

(i) Tort

7–106   NOTE 12: For para.7–089 read para.7–098.

(2) *Situations where the benefit is generally ignored*

(b) Other situations

(i) Other contracts

7–118   Add at the end of the paragraph: In *Earl's Terrace Properties Ltd v Nilsson Design Ltd* [2004] B.L.R. 273 the claimant company, suing its architect for delay in completion of a housing project, did not have to take into account in the damages claimed (details at para.26–008A, below) any increase in profit from the delayed sale of the houses on a rising market because the sale at higher prices was unconnected with the breach of contract which brought about the delay: see *ibid.* paras 99 to 108.

(ii) Tort

Insert new paragraphs after para.7–123:

7–123A   The result arrived at in *Barings plc v Coopers & Lybrand* [2003] Lloyd's Rep. I.R. 566, the basic facts of which are set out at para.4–018, above, is difficult to support in the light of the decisions in the text, decisions to which Evans-Lombe J. does not appear to have been directed. The losses resulting from the unauthorised trading of the claimants' fraudulent employee had been subject to very substantial fluctuations both before and after the time that it was held the unauthorised trading, and hence the losses, should have been detected by the claimants themselves. Evans-Lombe J., referring to this time as the cut-off date for the calculation of losses, being the time when the chain of causation was broken, held that, while the claimants could not increase their damages by claiming the highest amount to which the losses had climbed after the cut-off date, the defendants were nevertheless entitled to argue for the lowest amount to which the losses had fallen on the ground that the reduction in losses constituted a benefit to be taken into account.

7–123B   Yet surely the correct analysis, in line with the authorities, is that the loss to the claimants had crystallised at the cut-off date when the causative effect of the damage was held to have ended. From that date the claimants are to be regarded as being solely responsible for the losses. They are now considered to be fully in charge of the business and what they do with it is a matter for their business judgment; it is, as Robert Goff J. put it in *The Elena d'Amico* (at para.7–117 of the main text), "[their] own business decision independent of the wrong". The risk of an increase in losses therefore passed to the claimants and with it the benefit of a decrease. The fact that they may still not have known at the cut-off date of the unauthorised trading, and consequently of the defendants' breach of contract, may distinguish the case from the other authorities in the main text where at the time of crystallisation of loss the claimant knew of the loss and of the defendant's wrong; but this should not make a difference. Once the court has held that the chain of causation is broken, what is done in the future lies in the hands of the claimants. To hold otherwise would make a nonsense of the decision on causation, for if it were still possible to look to the extent of the losses at future dates, it would mean that cause was still operating against the defendants. Indeed logically it would allow increases in the losses to be taken into account, which Evans-Lombe J. was properly not prepared to allow, as well as decreases.

Evans-Lombe J.'s reasoning had gone along the following lines. He posited **7–123C** two hypothetical cut-off dates falling after the cut-off date he had himself chosen; the first fell at the time when the losses were at their highest, standing at some £84 million, the second fell two and a half months later when the losses had reduced to some £44 million. He then argued from these two positions that it would be odd if the defendants were required to pay less when it took the claimants longer to find out what their fraudulent employee had been doing. But this misses the point. A decision on the cut-off date is a decision on when the claimants ought fully to have known the position; there is no question of the claimants being more at fault the later they are taken to acquire the relevant knowledge. It is purely fortuitous whether the losses are at their low ebb or have reached their ceiling, or are somewhere in between, at the moment of cut-off.

However, as it happened, the level of losses at the time that the chain of **7–123D** causation was held to be broken was very near to the lowest to which the losses subsequently fell — some £27½ million as opposed to some £25 million — so that, by holding that the defendants' liability was to be calculated by reference to the £25 million, no great harm was done.

4. ACTIONS TAKEN AFTER THE WRONG BY THIRD PARTIES

(1) *The particular case of gratuitous assistance afforded to the physically injured*

Add at the end of the paragraph: The rule of no deduction from the dam- **7–127** ages in respect of gratuitous assistance afforded to the claimant was applied where the claim was other than for personal injury in *Hamilton-Jones v David & Snape* [2004] 1 W.L.R. 924. Neuberger J. rightly said that he could "see no reason, in logic or policy, as to why the principle should be limited", as was being contended, to personal injury claims. Rather it seemed to him that in essence "the principle can be said to be based on the proposition that the gratuitous payment of money by third parties to the claimant is *res inter alios* *acta*, as between the claimants and the defendants": *ibid.*, para.74. See the case further at para.7–131, below.

(3) *Miscellaneous situations*

7–131   Insert after the first sentence of the paragraph: *Hamilton-Jones v David & Snape* [2004] 1 W.L.R. 924 can be said to be a further case in the miscellaneous category of benefits provided by a third party not taken into account in the damages although the case simply represented an extension of the specific category (at para.7–127 of the main text) of gratuitous assistance afforded to the physically injured. The claimant, suing her solicitor for negligence in allowing her children to be removed to Tunisia by their Tunisian father, was awarded, *inter alia*, the substantial travel costs of visiting her children in Tunisia from time to time although these costs had been paid by her mother. Neuberger J., generalising the principle, said at *ibid.*, para.74: "There is no reason why payments made to the claimant by third parties, particularly when those payments are made out of natural love and affection for the claimant, should be credited to the benefit of the person whose negligence has harmed the claimant, and to the disadvantage of the claimant. Indeed, it would seem almost absurd if that were the law." See the case also at para.7–127, above.

5. ACTIONS TAKEN BEFORE THE WRONG BY THE CLAIMANT

(2) *Sub-contracts made before breach and carried out despite breach*

(a) Sale of goods

7–146   Substitute for "value of the goods as warranted and as" on the last line but five of the paragraph: value of the goods as warranted and as is.

CHAPTER 8

CERTAINTY OF DAMAGE

II. CIRCUMSTANCES IN WHICH DAMAGES MAY BE AWARDED ALTHOUGH THE NATURE OF THE DAMAGE PREVENTS ABSOLUTE CERTAINTY OF PROOF

3. WHERE IT IS UNCERTAIN HOW A PECUNIARY LOSS IS TO BE MEASURED

NOTE 26: Add at the end: See now *Giles v Rhind (No.2)* [2004] 1 B.C.L.C. **8–009** 385 where the claimant shareholder recovered in damages substantial amounts for loss of earnings and loss of value of his investment in the company. *Giles v Rhind* is now reported at [2003] Ch. 618, CA.

NOTE 28: Add at the end: For the method of valuation of a company, which presented a degree of uncertainty, see *Matlaszek v Bloom Camillin* [2004] P.N.L.R. 17, p.309 at para.29–009, n.35, below.

4. WHERE IT IS UNCERTAIN HOW MUCH OF THE LOSS, PECUNIARY OR NON-PECUNIARY, IS ATTRIBUTABLE TO THE DEFENDANT'S BREACH OF DUTY

Add at the end of the paragraph: *Rugby Joinery UK v Whitfield* [2005] **8–013** EWCA Civ 561, May 10, is a further case of apportionment, the condition being, as in *Allen* (in this para. in the main text), vibration white finger and the exposure being, as in *Crookall* and *Thompson* (main text para.8–011), between innocent and guilty on a time basis under a single employer. It was accepted that there should be apportionment, the issue being how apportionment should be worked out; straight line on a time basis was rejected as, in the circumstances, unfair to the claimant. On the other hand, in *Brookes v South Yorkshire Passenger Transport Executive* [2005] EWCA Civ 452, April 28, another vibration white finger case, full recovery was allowed with no apportionment since it was not shown that the innocent exposure had caused any damage to the claimant: see *ibid.*, at paras 24 to 27. Similarly, in *Hartman v South Essex Mental Health & Community Care NHS Trust* [2005] I.C.R. 782, CA, where there was psychiatric injury to one of the claimants from stress at work, apportionment was held inappropriate as it had not been shown by the employer, upon whom the burden lay, that the employee's illness was attributable in part to non-negligent stress: see *ibid.*, paras 119 to 124. And the Court of Appeal again recognised in *Harris v BRB Residuary Ltd* [2005] EWCA 900, July 18, a case like *Thompson* (at para.8–011 of the main text) of excessive noise at work causing deafness, that there could be apportionment of damages in appropriate circumstances, but none such had been either pleaded or proved by the employer defendant: see *ibid.*, paras 84 to 87.

8–014   NOTE 55: Add at the end: Nothing said at this point in *Hatton* is affected by *Barber v Somerset CC* [2004] 1 W.L.R. 1089, HL where the House of Lords allowed the further appeal of one of the appellants in four conjoined appeals which had been heard earlier in the Court of Appeal under the title *Hatton v Sutherland.*

Add at the end of the paragraph: However apportionment was rejected by the Court of Appeal in *Barker v Saint Gobain Pipelines plc* [2004] P.I.Q.R. P p.579, CA although the damages were reduced for contributory negligence. See the case at para.6–017, above.

5. WHERE IT IS UNCERTAIN WHETHER A PARTICULAR PECUNIARY LOSS WILL BE OR WOULD HAVE BEEN INCURRED

(1) *Prospective expenses*

8–018   Add at the end of the paragraph: In *Adan v Securicor Custodial Services Ltd* [2005] P.I.Q.R. P p.79 the court would not agree to postponing the adjudication of damages where there was a largely speculative chance that the injured claimant might cease to be mentally impaired and in the care of and at the expense of the State, and be returned to the community in need of extensive care and accommodation. Here the uncertainty was not as to the quantification of an established head of loss but as to whether the loss would come about at all: *ibid.*, para.23. It should be noted that in *A v National Blood Authority* (in this para. in the main text) the judge had taken the course of postponing assessment at the invitation of the parties: see *Adan* at paras 20 and 21.

Add a new note at the end of the paragraph:

NOTE 80a: In *Browning v Brachers* [2004] P.N.L.R. 28, p.517, where the damages included costs assessed some years earlier against the claimants in another action (facts at para.8–055C, below), costs that the claimants might never be required to pay as there had been no attempt at their enforcement to date, the court considered the best course was to order the defendant to indemnify the claimants should the costs be pursued and payment of them by the claimants follow. This holding was not challenged in the appeal: see [2005] EWCA Civ 753, June 20, at para.149.

(4) *Loss of a chance: chance dependent upon third parties*

(b) The range of the loss of a chance doctrine

(i) The distinction between past events and future events

Insert new paragraphs after para.8–032:

The House of Lords' affirmation in *Gregg v Scott* [2005] 2 A.C. 176, **8–032A** though only by a bare majority, of the Court of Appeal's decision, also by a majority, is a matter of the greatest importance for the law on loss of a chance, the implications of which cannot be fully explored in a Supplement. Consideration of the decision has to be taken in two stages. Only the second is, strictly speaking, concerned with loss of a chance but the first needs to be addressed in advance of turning to the second.

The first stage concerns what Lord Hoffmann at *ibid.*, para.67 calls the **8–032B** quantification argument. This is the argument referred to at para.8–031 of the main text as used by Latham L.J., dissenting in the Court of Appeal, in order to find for the claimant. Since, he argued, the nine-month delay in treatment had allowed the cancer to spread and the tumour to enlarge, this amounted to physical injury, and recovery for what he referred to as "the reduced prospects of successful treatment" ([2003] Lloyd's Rep. Med. 105, CA, para.41) could be allowed as consequential loss flowing from this established injury; so deciding, he found it unnecessary to decide the case on loss of a chance (also at para.41). The fact that there was no certainty about this consequential loss did not matter as, in quantifying loss, possibilities as well as probabilities can be taken into account. But, as Lord Hoffmann pointed out in his analysis of the quantification argument at paras 67 to 71, for loss to be recoverable it must be shown that the damage in question was attributable to the defendant's wrongful act. Thus where the claimant's hip is tortiously injured there can be recovery for the possibility that it will develop arthritis since the injury to the hip is attributable to, and caused by, the wrongful act; similarly, there was recovery in *Doyle v Wallace* [1998] P.I.Q.R. Q p.146, CA (at para.8–047 of the main text) for the possibility that the claimant would have had higher earnings had she qualified as a drama teacher since her loss of earnings was attributable to, and caused by, the defendant who injured her. In the instant case, however, it was necessary to show that the loss of life expectation claimed for was attributable to, and caused by, the defendant's negligence which had allowed the cancer to spread. This was not known and had not, as the trial judge had held, been proved. The controlling distinction has been best and most concisely formulated in a sentence cited approvingly by Lord Hoffmann in *Gregg v Scott* and earlier in Scotland in *Kenyon v Bell* 1953 S.C. 125, 128, a sentence of a Canadian judge, Master J., in *Kranz v McCutcheon* 18 Ont. W.N. 395 (1920): "The rule against recovery of uncertain damages is directed against uncertainty as to cause rather than as to extent or measure". The quantification argument therefore did not avail the claimant, and Lord Hope's introduction of *Doyle* and the related *Langford v Hebran* [2001] P.I.Q.R. Q p.160, CA (at para.8–048 of the main text) in support of his minority holding for the claimant ([2005] 2 A.C. 176, para.119) is misconceived.

8–032C   The second stage takes us to the loss of a chance proper. In essence the majority of their Lordships held that the loss of a chance doctrine had no application to cases of clinical negligence or indeed to personal injuries generally. Loss of a chance as established in the economic sphere was not to be extended to the physical sphere. The existing loss of a chance cases, the rationale of which was put on a firm footing by *Allied Maples* (see para.8–033 *et seq.* of the main text), is dependent upon human activity and human decisions which are in their very nature uncertain, and where such uncertainties come into the assessment of damages, the loss of a chance approach makes sense. By contrast, with physical injury there is no inherent uncertainty as to cause but only a lack of knowledge, and lack of knowledge is dealt with in the law by the burden of proof, so that it is appropriate to apply the balance of probabilities rule to the situation, an approach which will favour sometimes the defendant and, also, sometimes the claimant. While of course it may be said that this distinction, though not difficult to formulate, has only legal principle and legal consistency, and not fairness and justice, on its side, there are nevertheless sound, indeed vital, practical reasons for making it. Thus, as Baroness Hale asked ([2005] 2 A.C. 176, paras 222 to 225), where would extension of loss of a chance into the physical sphere stop? Would not every claimant be able to argue that he had, say, a 30 per cent chance of proving his case and therefore should be entitled to 30 per cent of the damages? Indeed, as Baroness Hale put it, if this were to be allowed, why should the claimant, though able to satisfy the court on the balance of probabilities test, not be restricted to the percentage of loss he could causatively prove? Such a development would play havoc with the rules on proof.

8–032D   The decision on loss of a chance is therefore to be commended. In particular, the controversial decision in *Hotson v East Berkshire Area Health Authority* (at para.8–029 of the main text) is vindicated. Indeed *Gregg v Scott* may well go further than *Hotson* in a defendant's favour. Thus, while of the House of Lords majority Lord Hoffmann considered that a decision for the claimant would require the overruling of *Hotson*, Baroness Hale thought that *Hotson* was distinguishable and could stand whichever way *Gregg* was decided: see *Gregg v Scott* at para.85 for Lord Hoffmann and at paras 210 to 212 for Baroness Hale, and see para.8–031 of the main text for similar disagreement in the Court of Appeal. As for the view of the minority that a failure to hold for the claimant in *Gregg v Scott* would constitute a wrong without a remedy — as stated by Lord Nicholls at paras 2 and 25 and by Lord Hope at para.106 — this begs the question. They assume that a wrong has been done. But that is the very question that it is for the court to decide: *has* a wrong been done?

(ii) Dependency upon acts of third parties

Insert at the beginning of the sixth line of the paragraph: House of Lords **8–033** affirming the

Insert a new note after the first sentence of the paragraph: **8–035**

NOTE 28a: Thus in *Floyd v. John Fairhurst & Co* [2004] P.N.L.R. 41, p.795, CA (facts at para.8–045, below) it was accepted on all sides that the claimant had to establish on the balance of probabilities what his own actions would have been.

(c) Particular cases

(i) Claims against solicitors

Insert a new note at the end of the paragraph: **8–038**

NOTE 43a: That loss of a chance applies as much to cases of negligent handling of litigation as to cases of negligent advice is confirmed by the Court of Appeal in *Dixon v Clement Jones Solicitors* [2004] EWCA Civ 1005, July 8, and further illustrated, again in the Court of Appeal, by *Browning v Brachers* [2005] EWCA Civ 753, June 20: see these cases at para.8–043A and paras 8–055A to 8–055D, below respectively.

Add at the end of the paragraph: The claim against the solicitor in **8–041** *Williams v Glyn Owen & Co* [2004] P.N.L.R. 20, p.367, CA was for failing to advise the claimant, buying a farm for its immediate stocking with breeding ewes, to serve a completion notice upon the vendor when it became apparent that the vendor would not be able to give vacant possession on the date fixed for completion and therefore not in time to allow stocking before the market for breeding ewes had disappeared. Although completion could not have taken place in time to catch the market even if a completion notice had been served, account had to be taken of the chance that, had a notice been served, the vendor would have agreed a date for completion which would have provided the claimant with sufficient assurance to enable him to purchase breeding stock. That chance being assessed by the Court of Appeal at 40 per cent, the claimant was held entitled to that percentage of the profit he would have made had he bought in time. And see too *Ball v Druces & Attlee (No.2)* [2004] P.N.L.R. 39, p.745 at para.29–031, below.

8–042   Add at the end of the paragraph: In *Maden v Clifford Coppock & Carter* [2005] P.N.L.R. 7, p.112, CA, where the solicitor's negligence was by wrongly advising on the costs consequences of litigation with a third party and the damages were dependent on the claimant having successfully settled this litigation (see the facts at para.29–024, below), the Court of Appeal held that the trial judge had been wrong to make no discount for the chance that the third party might not have agreed to a settlement, although the discount that the Court of Appeal decided upon was comparatively small, at 20 per cent.

Insert a new paragraph after para.8–043:

8–043A   *Dixon v Clement Jones Solicitors* [2004] EWCA Civ 1005, July 8, was a typical case of solicitors' negligence in the conduct of litigation in which it was attempted, unsuccessfully, to overturn a half century of authorities by the bold but misconceived argument that the loss of chance doctrine did not apply to such cases. The facts and outcome were run of the mill. Mrs Dixon's action against her accountants for negligently advising her over a business transaction was struck out for failure of her solicitors to serve a statement of claim, and in her action against her solicitors the judge assessed the chance of her having succeeded against her accountants at 30 per cent. Nevertheless it was contended for the defendant solicitors that the judge should have dismissed her claim against them because she could not show on the balance of probabilities that she would have won her case against her accountants. It was said that cases of solicitors' negligent conduct of litigation, as opposed to solicitors' negligence in acting in or advising on transactions, fall within the second of the three categories set out in *Allied Maples v Simmons & Simmons* [1995] 1 W.L.R. 1602, CA (for which see para.8–034 of the main text) rather than within the third, the difference between the two categories turning on whether causation depends on the hypothetical action, respectively, of the claimant, where balance of probabilities controls, or of a third party or parties, where loss of a chance reigns. The argument for the second category, as advanced by the defendant, would seem to be based on the fact that it is the claimant who was proceeding with the suit which is now lost and therefore it is a claimant's hypothetical action that is in issue. But this misses the point. What is in issue is not the bringing of the claim that is lost but its prospects of success, and that is indeed dependent not upon the claimant but on third parties. The third party would be the judge if the case were to go to trial and would be the other party to the lost claim if the case were to settle. "Ultimately", said Rix L.J. delivering the principal judgment, at *ibid.*, para.42,

> "the value of the underlying litigation did not lie in Mrs Dixon's own hands, but in the hands of the court (or, in the case of settlement, in the hands of bilateral negotiation)".

Moreover, as the Court of Appeal emphasised and as had been pointed out in earlier authorities, the court is not required to attempt itself to conduct a trial of the lost action — to fight out a trial within a trial — but to assess the chance of the claimant's having been successful in the action, or indeed in a settlement of it. As Rix L.J. rightly said, "it is the prospects and not the hypothetical decision in the lost trial that have to be investigated": *ibid.*, para.27.

(iii) Claims against other professional advisers

Add at the end of the paragraph: In *John D Wood & Co (Residential and Agricultural) v Knatchbull* [2003] 1 E.G.L.R. 33 the defendant estate agent, who had been instructed by the claimant to find a buyer for his property with the asking price set at £1.5 million, failed to inform the claimant that the asking price for a similar neighbouring property was £1.95 million, and damages were awarded the claimant for loss of the chance of selling at a figure higher than his asking price. In *University of Keele v Price Waterhouse* [2004] P.N.L.R. 8, p.112 a university, which wished to set up a tax-efficient profit-related pay scheme for its employees, was wrongly advised by the defendant accountants as to the number of participating employees required for the scheme to be valid, with the result that the scheme failed and the university had to pay substantial amounts in tax to the Inland Revenue, amounts which it sought to recover as damages from the defendants. It was held that the proper approach to the damages was to consider the chance that the university would have had, if it had been properly advised, to achieve the required number of employee participants. The court assessed the chances of success at 80 per cent, thereby entitling the university to recover 80 per cent of the moneys it had paid over in tax. No damages issue appears in the appeal: [2004] P.N.L.R. 43, p.888, CA. *Floyd v John Fairhurst & Co* [2004] P.N.L.R. 41, p.795, CA also involved a negligent accountant and tax adviser. When advising the claimant in relation to a compulsory purchase of his land, the tax adviser failed to inform the claimant of the availability of so-called roll-over relief against capital gains tax if he reinvested his compensation in replacement qualifying assets. Since it was accepted that the claimant had to show not simply that he had lost the chance of taking advantage of roll-over relief but that on the balance of probabilities he would have done so (*ibid.*, para.10) and since the trial judge and the Court of Appeal both held that he had failed in this, his claim necessarily failed. Nonetheless both courts considered the damages to which the claimant would have been entitled had he satisfied them that he would have utilised the roll-over relief. The various heads are considered very fully and fairly in Arden L.J.'s leading judgment but of course they no longer require to be estimated as loss of a chance damages. In *Francis v Barclay Bank plc* [2005] P.N.L.R. 18, p.297 the negligent advice was that of a surveyor. A bank's sale of land to a company provided that, if the company sold the land with planning permission for residential development within 10 years, the bank would be entitled to half of the price at which the company sold. About a year after the sale by the bank the company offered it an immediate £25,000 if it would limit its future entitlement to £75,000.

8–045

The bank would only agree to this if it regarded it as unlikely that the planning status of the land would change and be brought within the boundary for permitting residential development. The bank consulted the surveyor as to the prospects of such re-designation and the surveyor negligently advised that the prospects were slim. Accordingly the bank accepted the company's offer, the land was duly re-designated, planning permission was obtained and the company sold for over £2 million. The surveyor argued that his negligence had caused the bank no loss as the company would have deferred sale with planning permission until the 10-year period had elapsed, thereby entitling the bank to no part of the company's selling price. The trial judge held however that it was twice as likely that the company would have gone ahead with the sale, as it did, and not have awaited the expiry of the 10 years; this represented the lost chance.

(iv) Personal injury claims

Insert a new paragraph after para.8–049:

8–049A   The correctness of the argument in the text that *Doyle v Wallace* [1998] P.I.Q.R. Q p.146, CA and *Langford v Hebran* [2001] P.I.Q.R. Q p.160, CA are not to be seen as cases of loss of a chance in the correct sense of that term is made abundantly clear by Lord Hoffmann in *Gregg v Scott* [2005] 2 A.C. 176. This is fully explained at para.8–032B, above. And issues involving lost chances of earnings and concerning loss of a chance proper are neatly juxtaposed in *Luke v Wansbroughs* [2005] P.N.L.R. 2, p.15 where the claimant, who had been a non-commissioned soldier in the army, sued his solicitor and barrister for negligence in having settled at an alleged undervalue his claim against three army officers for malicious falsehood that had brought his army career to an abrupt end. While Davis J. exonerated both solicitor and barrister of negligence, he dealt, as a coda to his judgment, with the damages that would have been recoverable had liability been found. For the purpose of arriving at the loss of earnings in the malicious falsehood claim he assessed the claimant's chances of becoming commissioned to the rank of captain, had he remained in the army, at 15 per cent and then went on to assess his chances of winning the malicious falsehood claim, which he placed at 35 per cent. Only the latter was regarded by him as giving rise to loss of a chance: see *ibid.*, paras 121 to 126.

8–050   Add at the end of the paragraph: No change here has in fact been made by the House of Lords' ruling in *Gregg v Scott* [2005] 2 A.C. 176: see paras 8–032A to 8–032D, above.

(vi) Claims arising in connection with contracts of employment

8–052   NOTE 12: Add at the end: *Harper v Virgin Net Ltd* [2004] I.R.L.R. 390, CA establishes that an employee suing for damages for summary wrongful dismissal without the contractual notice to which she was entitled cannot claim for the loss of a chance of recovering compensation for unfair dismissal on the basis that by the end of the contractual notice, but not by the end of the statutory notice to which entitled under the unfair dismissal provisions, she would have had the necessary qualifying service to support a claim for unfair dismissal. Properly analysed, there was no loss of a chance. The employee did not lose her right to claim for unfair dismissal as she never had such a right; she fell short of the length of continuous service prescribed by the legislature as the gateway to such a right. *cf.* especially Chadwick L.J.'s judgment at *ibid.*, paras 25 and 26. *Harper* was applied in *Wise Group v Mitchell* [2005] I.C.R. 896, EAT.

(c) Assessment of the value of the lost chance

(i) Where the chance relates to success in a damages claim

Insert new paragraphs after para.8–055:

Mount also laid down further propositions — all are in the judgment of Simon Brown L.J. at [1998] P.N.L.R. 493, 510, CA — adverse to defendant solicitors. He said first that, if the court now has greater difficulty in discerning the strength of the claimant's original claim, or defence, than it would have had at the time of the original action, such difficulty should not count against him but rather against his negligent solicitors. Secondly, he said that generally speaking, when evaluating the claimant's chances of success, one would expect the court to tend towards a generous assessment given that it was the defendant's negligence which lost the claimant the opportunity of succeeding in full or fuller measure. And the most recent consideration of the advantageous position of a claimant in a loss of a chance case appears in *Browning v Brachers* [2005] EWCA Civ 753, June 20, bringing in, as have earlier cases there cited, the well-known and, though old, still important decision in *Armory v Delamirie* (1722) 1 Strange 505 (considered in a somewhat different context at para.33–047 of the main text). Jonathan Parker L.J., giving the only reasoned judgment with which the others agreed, there said, at *ibid.*, para.210, that the principle in *Armory v Delamirie* (the impact of which case he considered generally at paras 204 to 213), **8–055A**

> "raises an evidential (i.e. rebuttable) presumption in favour of the claimant which gives him the benefit of any relevant doubt. The practical effect of that is to give the claimant a fair wind in establishing the value of what he has lost."

Moreover, as has now been emphasised by the Court of Appeal in *Dixon v Clement Jones Solicitors* [2004] EWCA Civ 1005, July 8 (at para.8–043A, above) and again in *Browning v Brachers* [2005] EWCA Civ 753, June 20 (at para.8–055C, below), it is not the task of the court to attempt to conduct a trial of the lost action but simply to assess its prospects of success. Nevertheless in *Browning v Brachers* somewhat different results were arrived **8–055B** at by the trial judge and by the Court of Appeal: [2004] P.N.L.R. 28, p.517 and [2005] EWCA Civ 753, June 20.

8–055C   In that case the seller of a goat-farming business had brought an action against the buyers alleging that part of the price had not been paid and the buyers counterclaimed for lost profits alleging that the goatherd sold to them had infected their own herd. The buyers' side of the litigation was handled so badly by their solicitor that the counterclaim was dismissed with costs; at about the same time the seller's claim was settled. In the buyers' successful action against their solicitor for professional negligence the trial judge applied what he called a broad brush approach without attempting to retry the putative action itself. He made estimates of what the buyers would have been awarded for loss of profits and of what the seller would have been awarded for unpaid price had their respective claims succeeded and then applied discounts of 30 per cent and 25 per cent respectively to take account of the chance of failure. In the Court of Appeal, while there was no dispute about the 30 per cent liability discount — indeed there was no appeal about it (see [2005] EWCA Civ 753, para.24) — the buyers' damages were substantially increased because the judge's estimates of their potential loss of profits had been ungenerous and faulty: see the issues in the appeal set out at *ibid.*, para.154 and the Court of Appeal's conclusions on all these matters at *ibid.*, paras 214 to 236. As for the 25 per cent discount which had brought the seller's very small claim for unpaid price down from the £8,000s to the £6,000s (see *ibid.*, paras 10 and 143), this went out of the window as the Court of Appeal held that the proper figure to take was the £5,000 at which the seller's claim had been earlier settled: see *ibid.*, paras 237 and 259.

8–055D   In addition, the trial judge held the buyers entitled to damages in respect of the costs payable by them to the seller in respect of the unsuccessful counterclaim; a discount of 25 per cent was applied here to cater for the fact that, even if the buyers had been successful, some part of the costs of their counterclaim could well have been disallowed (see [2004] P.N.L.R. 28, p.517, para.96). This aspect of the case, upon which there was no appeal (see [2005] EWCA Civ 753, para.149), may or may not be regarded as concerning the loss of a chance.

8–057   Add at the end of the paragraph: *Charles v Hugh Jenkins & Jones* [2000] 1 W.L.R. 1278, CA has been criticised in Scotland at first instance in *Campbell v Imray* [2004] P.N.L.R. 1, p.1, a similar solicitor's negligence case, although Lord Emslie had no need to apply it as he was finding for the defendant and in any case was of the view that *Charles* did not actually decide that unforeseeable events subsequent to the notional trial date could be taken into account: see *ibid.*, para.48. He said, at *ibid.*, para.49:

> "In the absence of clear and compelling authority, I would not have been disposed to assess damages for a 'lost' action by reference to matters which could not have been known or foreseen at the notional trial or

settlement date. Suppose A and B suffer substantially the same injuries in the same accident caused by the same wrongdoer: can it really be right that A, whose action is lost through his solicitors' professional negligence, may end up with a claim substantially higher, or substantially lower, than B whose claim is timeously raised? And what if it is held that A's claim would probably have been settled extra-judicially: is that settlement to be judged by reference to matters of which neither party could possibly have been aware at the material time? Further, suppose that two wrongdoers are jointly and severally liable for the same pursuer's loss, and proceedings are timeously commenced against one but not against the other: can the notional liability of the latter, assessed in professional negligence proceedings, seriously be taken at a level bearing no resemblance to the liability of the former? Such questions, as it seems to me, must logically be answered in the negative if comparative justice is to be maintained, and if the true purpose of an award of damages is to restore a pursuer, so far as monetary payment can do so, to the position in which he would have been if the wrong complained of had not occurred".

Add at the end of the paragraph: The same method is to be used — and **8–058** was used in *Sharpe v Addison* [2004] P.N.L.R. 23, p.426, CA — where two discounts have to be made not in respect of two aspects of the chance of success of the damages claim but in respect of the chance of success and the chance that the damages would have been reduced for contributory negligence. In *Sharpe*, where contributory negligence in the personal injury claim was assessed at 75 per cent and the chance of that claim succeeding at 40 per cent, the Court of Appeal first discounted by 75 per cent and then discounted the remaining 25 per cent by 60 per cent, producing a total discount of 90 per cent and an expected recovery of 10 per cent. Here it would clearly have been nonsense to add the two discounts together as this would have taken the total discount to well over 100 per cent. See the analysis by Rix L.J. at *ibid.*, paras 30 to 35, where the calculation is done somewhat differently but achieves the result as set out above.

(5) *Loss of a chance: chance dependent upon the defendant*

Add at the end of the paragraph: In *Horkulak v Cantor Fitzgerald* **8–060** *International* [2003] I.C.R. 697, a case of wrongful dismissal involving breach of the implied term of trust and confidence, the claimant employee's contract provided that, if the financial results of the defendant employing company should follow a particular pattern, the company was entitled to reduce the employee's salary by up to 25 per cent. The financial results being such as to entitle the company to make the reduction, it was held, citing *Withers* and *Beach*, that the damages must be calculated on the basis of a salary reduced by the whole 25 per cent: see *ibid.*, para.87. On the appeal — [2005] I.C.R. 402, CA — this result was not challenged; for the aspect of the damages with which the appeal was concerned see paras 28–007A and 28–007B, below.

NOTE 42: Insert after the sentence dealing with *Morran v Glasgow Council of Tenants Associations*: This result is confirmed for England by *Harper v Virgin Net Ltd* [2004] I.R.L.R. 390, CA; see the case at para.8–052, n.12, above.

8–062   NOTE 48: Insert after the first sentence of the note: If as events have turned out the contract would have been brought to an end by the repudiating party before its due date even if the event triggering the termination was neither predestined nor inevitable at the date of repudiation, the damages are still to be limited accordingly. It was rightly so held in *The Golden Victory* [2005] 1 Lloyd's Rep. 443, another case of repudiatory breach of a charterparty by the charterer. The charter was for a seven-year period and at repudiation had nearly four more years to run. The owners claimed the normal measure of damages based upon the difference between the charter rate and the lower market rate for this period but, because the charterers would have been entitled to cancel on the outbreak of the war between the UK and Iraq some 14 months after the repudiation, the owners' claim for damages ran only for this shorter period.

NOTE 49: Add at the end: See too *Northern Foods plc v Focal Foods Ltd* [2003] 2 Lloyd's Rep. 728 where *The Mihalis Angelos* was invoked in support of limiting the claimant buyers to nominal damages: see *ibid.*, para.10.

8–063   Add at the end of the paragraph: In *Horkulak v Cantor Fitzgerald International* [2005] I.C.R. 402, CA it was held that a reasonable and bona fide performance of a contractual obligation to pay to an employee a bonus which was discretionary required that the bonus be paid; on this see the case at para.28–007A and 28–007B, below.

PAST AND PROSPECTIVE DAMAGE

I. INTRODUCTORY: CIRCUMSTANCES IN WHICH THE SAME SET OF FACTS GIVES RISE TO MORE THAN ONE CAUSE OF ACTION

4. WHERE A SINGLE ACT NOT ACTIONABLE *PER SE* CAUSES SEPARATE DAMAGE ON TWO SEPARATE OCCASIONS

NOTE 64: Add at the end: *Darley Main* was successfully prayed in aid in the unusual case of *Phonographic Performance Ltd v Department of Trade and Industry* [2004] 1 W.L.R. 2893 involving breach of statutory duty in the field of copyright (see *ibid.*, para.17 *et seq.*) but not in the further curious case of *Iqbal v Legal Services Commission* [2005] EWCA Civ 623, May 10, involving alleged breach of statutory duty and misfeasance in public office in withholding legal aid board funds from the claimant (see *ibid.*, para.19 *et seq.*).

9–014

II. PAST LOSS: DAMAGE BEFORE ACCRUAL OF THE CAUSE OF ACTION

NOTE 72: Add: *Rugby Joinery UK v Whitfield* [2005] EWCA Civ 561, May 10, is a further case along the same lines. But for apportionment it must be shown that the innocent exposure contributed to the injury: *Brookes v South*

9–016

Yorkshire Passenger Transport Executive [2005] EWCA Civ 452, April 28; *Hartman v South Essex Mental Health & Community Care NHS Trust* [2005] I.C.R. 782, CA; *Harris v BRB Residuary Ltd* [2005] EWCA 900, July 18. See these cases at para.8–013, above.

III. PAST LOSS: DAMAGE BEFORE COMMENCEMENT OF THE ACTION

9–023 NOTE 6: Add to the cases cited: *Rugby Joinery UK v Whitfield* [2005] EWCA Civ 561, May 10.

IV. PROSPECTIVE LOSS: DAMAGE AFTER COMMENCEMENT OF THE ACTON

2. THE COROLLARY

(1) *Where there is a single cause of action*

9–033 Add at the end of the paragraph: but not where the loss may not come about at all: see *Adan v Securicor Custodial Services Ltd* [2005] P.I.Q.R. P p.79 at para.8–018, above.

BOOK ONE

PART THREE

DAMAGES NOT BASED STRICTLY ON COMPENSATION

CHAPTER 10

NOMINAL DAMAGES

I. CIRCUMSTANCES GIVING RISE TO AN AWARD OF NOMINAL DAMAGES

1. WHERE THERE IS *INJURIA SINE DAMNO*

NOTE 3: Insert after the first line: See in *Watkins v Secretary of State for the*   **10–002**
Home Department [2005] 2 W.L.R. 1538, CA the wide-ranging learned discussion of the authorities, starting with the 300-year-old *Ashby v White* (at
para.10–003 of the main text), on what constitutes for the purpose of nominal damages torts which are and torts which are not actionable *per se*. The
tort of misfeasance in public office which had there been committed — by
prison officers interfering with a prisoner's correspondence — was held by
the Court of Appeal to be actionable *per se*.

Insert a new note before the last sentence of the paragraph: **10–003**

NOTE 6a: The discussion in *Watkins v Secretary of State for the Home
Department* [2005] 2 W.L.R. 1538, CA (see para.10–002, n.3, above) does not
really get to grips with the distinction between these two types of case.

II. AMOUNT AWARDED: NOMINAL AND SMALL DAMAGES DISTINGUISHED

NOTE 16: Add at the end: *Watkins v Secretary of State for the Home*   **10–006**
Department [2005] 2 W.L.R. 1538, CA.

Insert a new note after the third last sentence of the paragraph:

NOTE 18a: In one case the token sum awarded to each of the two claimants for breach of the Data Protection Act 1998 was £50: see *Douglas v Hello! Ltd (No.5)* [2003] E.M.L.R. 31, p.641 at para.239 and *Douglas v Hello! Ltd (No.6)* [2004] E.M.L.R. 2, p.13 at para.12.

III. PRACTICAL FUNCTIONS OF NOMINAL DAMAGES

10–009   Insert a new note after the first sentence of the paragraph:

NOTE 30a: And nominal damages can also be a peg on which to hang exemplary damages: *Watkins v Secretary of State for the Home Department* [2005] 2 W.L.R. 1538, CA.

CHAPTER 11

EXEMPLARY DAMAGES

I. THE GENERAL BAN ON EXEMPLARY DAMAGES

Insert a new note at the end of the paragraph: **11–007**

NOTE 38a: In *The Gleaner Co Ltd v Abrahams* [2004] 1 A.C. 628, PC the judgment of their Lordships' Board delivered by Lord Hoffmann may be read as being rather sympathetic to exemplary damages although it was with compensatory damages that their Lordships were there concerned. For the case further see para.1–002, above and *cf.* para.39–025, below.

II. CASES IN WHICH EXEMPLARY DAMAGES MAY BE AWARDED

1. TYPES OF CLAIM IN WHICH EXEMPLARY DAMAGES ARE POSSIBLE

Insert a new note at the end of the paragraph: **11–011**

NOTE 45a: Including torts based upon breach of statutory duty, as in *Design Progression Ltd v Thurloe Properties Ltd* [2005] 1 W.L.R. 1 (facts at para.11–025, below).

11–012   Insert a new note before the last sentence of the paragraph:

NOTE 47a: The tort of misfeasance in public office also attracted exemplary damages in *Watkins v Secretary of State for the Home Department* [2005] 2 W.L.R. 1538, CA.

11–015   NOTE 65: Add at the end: In *Re Organ Retention Group Litigation* [2005] Q.B. 506, a claim in negligence by parents in respect of the removal and retention of their deceased children's organs by the defendants, no exemplary award was made where the conduct of the defendants did not come anywhere near to being sufficiently outrageous or oppressive; the judge's assumption, without decision, that exemplary damages could be available in negligence claims was hardly necessary: see *ibid.*, para.263.

2. THE THREE CATEGORIES IN WHICH EXEMPLARY AWARDS ARE POSSIBLE

(1) *First common law category: oppressive, arbitrary or unconstitutional conduct by government servants*

11–018   NOTE 81: Add at the end: In *Reynolds* the exemplary award which the Privy Council was upholding was at common law for the false imprisonment and not for the breach, also present, of the claimant's constitutional rights, whereas the redress sanctioned by the Privy Council in *Attorney General of Trinidad and Tobago v Ramanoop* [2005] 2 W.L.R. 1324, PC was for the latter only and, although the award vindicating the claimant's infringed constitutional right would have much the same effect in financial terms as exemplary damages, it was not to be so described: see *ibid.*, para.19. Accordingly, *Ramanoop* falls outside the ambit of this text.

Add at the end of the paragraph: And misconduct by prison officers, by interfering with a prisoner's correspondence, featured in *Watkins v Secretary of State for the Home Department* [2005] 2 W.L.R. 1538, CA, allowing an exemplary award.

11–020   Insert a new note at the end of the paragraph:

NOTE 2a: In *Re Organ Retention Group Litigation* [2005] Q.B. 506 the judge, rightly or wrongly, seems to have taken a National Health Service Trust to be within this first category as he decided that the facts did not bring the claim within the criteria set out in *Rookes v Barnard* [1964] A.C. 1129. See the case at para.11–015, n.65, above.

(2) *Second common law category: conduct calculated to result in profit*

(a) Application by the courts

Add at the end of the paragraph: Again with a view to achieving a higher **11–025** rent of the property, the landlord in *Design Progression Ltd v Thurloe Properties Ltd* [2005] 1 W.L.R. 1, in breach of its statutory duty to respond in a reasonable time to its tenant's application for a licence to assign, had pursued a deliberately obstructive policy designed to prevent the assignment so that it could recover the premises with a view to granting a fresh lease at the full market rent. Exemplary damages were awarded.

(b) Scope, criticism and rationale

Insert a new paragraph after para.11–027:

That in second category cases the law is concerned more with profit than **11–027A** with punishment has now been underlined by the interesting, and in the circumstances of the case clearly correct, decision in *Borders (UK) Ltd v Commissioner of Police of the Metropolis* [2005] EWCA Civ 197, March 3. A street trader, who was there the second defendant, had run a racket selling stolen books on a massive scale until eventually apprehended; he was then prosecuted, was given a 30-month prison sentence and was facing a confiscation of proceeds of crime order. A consortium of booksellers, who were the claimants, had through the second defendant's activities lost probably a quarter of a million books, some 50,000 of which had been traced and retrieved. While the consortium claimed compensatory damages in respect of their losses on the retrieved books, for which they were awarded £280,000, they also claimed exemplary damages on account of a portion of their losses, and the second defendant's consequent profits, on the remaining and unretrieved books, for which they were awarded £100,000. The second defendant's argument that this latter award lay outside the court's powers since it constituted an amount which neither was compensatory, since it was pleaded as punitive, nor was punitive, since it represented actual losses, was not accepted. It was held to be entirely appropriate to make an exemplary award where the necessary conditions for one were made out, which they clearly were here, and the fact that the claimants had sought to justify the award of exemplary damages by reference to facts which could have sustained an award of further compensatory damages did not stand in the way. The court was also satisfied that the impending confiscation of proceeds of crime order would not expose the second defendant to double jeopardy as the order would take into account the exemplary award in the civil proceedings, and the £100,000 would therefore go to the claimants rather than to the State.

III. THE AMOUNT OF THE EXEMPLARY AWARD

1. VARIOUS CRITERIA APPLIED BY THE COURTS

(2) *Moderation in awards*

11–036   NOTE 86: Add at the end: See *Design Progression Ltd v Thurloe Properties Ltd* [2005] 1 W.L.R. 1, where the claim against the landlord was not by reason of the tenant's eviction but on account of blocking the assignment of the tenant's lease (facts at para.11–025, above), the award was higher still, at £25,000. "'Moderate' ... is to be assessed", said Peter Smith J. at *ibid.*, para.150, "in the overall facts of the case and in the light of the conduct and the need to mark disapproval."

(5) *The relevance of the amount awarded as compensation*

11–040   Add at the end of the paragraph: That the compensatory damages were sufficiently high to afford adequate punishment of the defendant appears as the justification of no award of exemplary damages by the Jamaican courts in *The Gleaner Co Ltd v Abrahams* [2004] 1 A.C. 628, PC. There was no claimant's appeal on this to the Privy Council but it is certainly how the position was regarded by Lord Hoffmann, giving the Board's judgment on the defendant's appeal: see *ibid.*, paras 40 and 41. By contrast, exemplary damages were awardable in *Watkins v Secretary of State for the Home Department* [2005] 2 W.L.R. 1538, CA where the compensatory damages were only nominal, at £5: see at *ibid.*, para.61.

(6) *The relevance of any criminal penalty*

11–041   Add at the end of the paragraph: That the prosecution, conviction and imprisonment of the defendant does not, with a profit-motivated tort, preclude an exemplary damages award of substantial proportions against him is well illustrated by *Borders (UK) Ltd v Commissioner of Police of the Metropolis* [2005] EWCA Civ 197, March 3 (facts at para.11–027A, above).

(9) *The question of vicarious liability*

11–045   Insert a new note on the ninth line before the reference to Lord Scott:

NOTE 37a: In *Watkins v Secretary of State for the Home Department* [2005] 2 W.L.R. 1538, CA the claimant did ask for exemplary damages against the individual actors (prison officers) and also thought it politic, in the light of Lord Scott's comments in *Kuddus* (see para.11–044 of the main text), not to press for an exemplary award against their superior (the Home Office): see at *ibid.*, paras 54 and 55.

2. THE IRRELEVANCE OF THE CRITERIA TO THE SECOND COMMON LAW CATEGORY

NOTE 43: Add at the end: But the criteria can be relevant where the defendant's design to achieve profits has failed, as in *Design Progression Ltd v Thurloe Properties Ltd* [2005] 1 W.L.R. 1 (facts at para.11–025, above). **11–046**

NOTE 45: Add at the end: The irrelevance of any criminal penalty (*cf.* para.11–041 of the main text) is illustrated by *Borders (UK) Ltd v Commissioner of Police of the Metropolis* [2005] EWCA Civ 197, March 3 (facts at para.11–027A, above).

CHAPTER 12

RESTITUTIONARY DAMAGES

II. CIRCUMSTANCES GIVING RISE TO RESTITUTIONARY DAMAGES

1. LIABILITY IN TORT

12–010   Add at the end of the paragraph: But the Court of Appeal has continued to base recovery on lost user and lost bargaining opportunity in *Severn Trent Water Ltd v Barnes* [2004] EWCA Civ 570, May 13: see the case at paras 34–052A to 34–052C, below.

(1) *Torts affecting property*

(a) Wrongful interference with land

(ii) Wrongful interference involving easements

12–013   Insert in the text before the penultimate sentence of the paragraph: A further case of a similar nature, but involving the laying of a water main rather than the erection of a building, is *Severn Trent Water Ltd v Barnes* [2004] EWCA Civ 570, May 13: see the case at paras 34–052A to 34–052C, below.

2. LIABILITY IN CONTRACT

(1) *The three key authorities*

(a) *Wrotham Park Estate Co v Parkside Homes*

Add at the end of the paragraph: *Lane v O'Brien Homes* [2004] EWHC 303   **12–023**
(QB), February 5, which is a further decision following and applying
Wrotham Park, still tends to look at the damages awarded as compensatory,
as being for the loss of a bargaining opportunity. Yet in the particular circumstances of the case, where the potential of the property was not fully
appreciated at the time of contracting, the award is much more simply
explained along restitutionary lines: see this aspect of *Lane* at para.22–053B,
below.

CHAPTER 13

LIQUIDATED DAMAGES

1. HISTORICAL DEVELOPMENT OF LIQUIDATED DAMAGES AND PENALTIES

(4) *The modern law*

13–008   NOTE 31: Add at the end: The argument advanced in *Jeancharm Ltd (t/a Beaver International) v Barnet Football Club Ltd* (2004) 93 Con.L.R. 26, CA that Lord Dunedin's approach had been abandoned in *Philips Hong Kong* was roundly dismissed by the Court of Appeal: see para.13–014A, below.

2. THE NATURE AND EFFECT OF LIQUIDATED DAMAGES AND PENALITIES

(1) *Nature: genuine pre-estimate of damages as against a sum fixed* in terrorem

13–012   NOTE 48: Add at the end: Also *Murray v Leisureplay plc* [2005] EWCA Civ 963, July 28; see para.13–014E, below.

13–014   NOTE 54: Add: In the light of the main text here, see the various considerations taken into account in *Alfred McAlpine Capital Projects Ltd v Tilebox Ltd* [2005] B.L.R. 271 at para.94 in holding the specified sum there to be liquidated damages and not a penalty; facts at para.13–062, n.84, below.

Insert new paragraphs after para.13–014:

13–014A   It was however contended by the claimant in *Jeancharm Ltd (t/a Beaver International) v Barnet Football Club Ltd* (2004) 93 Con.L.R. 26, CA that *Philips Hong Kong* had departed from *Dunlop* and that it is no longer necessary to find a genuine pre-estimate of loss before holding a provision constitutes liquidated damages; we had moved on and all that now has to be done is to look at the contract as a whole whenever the parties are of equal bargaining power, as they were in *Jeancharm*. The Court of Appeal disagreed. All that had changed with *Philips Hong Kong* is that, in continuing to apply *Dunlop*, one should be careful in deciding, when parties are of equal bargaining power, whether the clause is a penalty: see at para.15. The rule in *Dunlop* had not been abandoned and it was clear, as Keene L.J. said at *ibid.*, para.21, that the Privy Council in *Philips Hong Kong* recognised "that the situation where one party is dominant is not exhaustive of those contracts where a penalty may be identified".

Jeancharm concerned a contract for the supply of football kit to the defendant club in which it was provided that invoices not paid by the club within 45 days of being rendered were to be paid with interest at the rate of 5 per cent per week, a rate which perhaps at first glance appears innocuous but which, translated to an annual rate, comes out at 260 per cent. There were also some very severe provisions in the contract which applied to the suppliers in the event of breach by them. The Court of Appeal had no difficulty in deciding that the interest provision constituted a penalty as it went far beyond anything that could conceivably be a reasonable pre-estimate of loss.

13–014B

An important decision of the Court of Appeal re-examining the whole issue of liquidated damages and penalties has now appeared and just in time for this Supplement; it is *Murray v Leisureplay plc* [2005] EWCA Civ 963, July 28. Starting from the observations of Mance L.J. in *Cine Bes Filmcilik Ve Yapimcilik v United International Pictures* [2003] EWCA Civ 1669, November 21 (itself not a decision between liquidated damages and penalty but a summary judgment case involving no more than the identification of a triable issue) that the language of stipulations *in terrorem* sounds unusual to modern ears, it was agreed that the time had come to recast the test in terms more suitable for today, and this recasting was to be found in the judgment of Colman J. in *Lordsvale Finance plc v Bank of Zambia* [1996] Q.B. 752 (now referred to at para.13–100, below) in a passage, at *ibid.*, 762G, cited with approval both by Mance L.J. in *Cine* and by all three members of the court in *Murray* to the effect that:

13–014C

> "whether a provision is to be treated as a penalty is a matter of construction to be resolved by asking whether at the time the contract was entered into the predominant contractual function of the provision was to deter a party from breaking the contract or to compensate the innocent party for breach".

In *Murray* the issue of liquidated damages or penalty arose in the context of a contract of employment. The claimant, employed as chief executive director of the defendant company, had a service agreement under which he was entitled to a year's notice and in which it was stipulated that, should the employer wrongfully terminate the contract by giving no notice or too little notice, the employee became entitled to a year's gross salary, pension and

13–014D

other benefits in kind. Stanley Burnton J. held that this provision constituted a penalty, being primarily influenced by the fact that it failed to take into account, and to make any allowance for, mitigation from other employment during the notice year. The Court of Appeal reversed.

13–014E   For the future of the law in this somewhat exceptional area of damages, it is important to look at the reasoning behind this decision in favour of liquidated damages. While the result was reached by a unanimous Court of Appeal, different approaches as to how this was to be achieved were taken by Arden L.J. on the one hand and by Buxton L.J. on the other, with Clarke L.J. expressing a preference for the broader approach of Buxton L.J. Although Arden L.J. came to the conclusion that the contractual provision was not a penalty, she could be said to have done so by adopting the conventional approach which requires a comparison between the amount put forward as liquidated damages and common law damages and, if there was a discrepancy, requires a justification of it. Buxton L.J. however considered that this introduced "a rigid and inflexible element into what should be a broad and general question": *ibid.*, para.114. Citing Lord Dunedin's test of extravagance and unconscionability for ascertaining a penal sum (at para.13–024 of the main text), he said that it was clear that neither the literal wording nor the spirit of the test applied to the case before the court: *ibid.*, para.115. Indeed for him the general impression created by it was that

> "the traditional learning as to penalty clauses is very unlikely to fit into the dynamics of an employment contract, at least when the penalty is said to be imposed on the employer": *ibid.*, para.115.

The judgments also laid emphasis on the rule that the burden of proof lies on the party seeking to escape liability to show that the particular provision is a penalty, it not being for the other party to justify it: Arden L.J. at *ibid.*, para.69 and Clarke L.J. at *ibid.*, para.106(vii) and (xi).

(2) *Effect of holding a stipulated sum to be liquidated damages or a penalty*

(a) Sum held to be liquidated damages

13–016   Insert a new note at the end of the fifth line after "stipulated sum":

NOTE 57a: It was however held in *Bath and North East Somerset DC v Mowlem* [2004] B.L.R. 153, CA that, where the actual loss is, or is likely to be, greater than the liquidated damages, this may be used as an argument for specific relief — in *Mowlem* by way of an injunction — on the ground that damages would not be an adequate remedy, and further that it is legitimate, in deciding on adequacy of remedy, to consider losses which would be irrecoverable, perhaps because too remote, as well as recoverable losses. Mance L.J. said:

"The Council accepts — indeed it asserts — that it would be bound in any claim for damages by its contractual agreement regarding liquidated and ascertained damages. The Council is not seeking to avoid that agreement but to rely on it. It is the reason the Council seeks an injunction": *ibid.*, para.15.

Insert a new note after the first sentence of the paragraph: **13–018**

NOTE 74a: Also he can support his claim for an injunction by reliance on the liquidated damages being lower than his actual loss: *Bath and North East Somerset DC v Mowlem* [2004] B.L.R. 153, CA, at para.13–016, n.57a, above.

3. RULES FOR DISTINGUISHING LIQUIDATED DAMAGES FROM PENALTIES

(3) *A stipulated sum is a penalty if it is extravagant and unconscionable in comparison with the greatest loss that could conceivably be proved to have followed from the breach: otherwise it is liquidated damages*

(b) Where there are several obligations upon the breach of which the sum becomes payable

(ii) Where the loss is not reasonably calculable at the time of contracting

NOTE 81: Add: But nothing in what Lord Woolf said is to be construed as **13–044** affecting the time-honoured rule that to avoid being held to be a penalty the agreed sum or sums must be a genuine pre-estimate of loss, as *Jeancharm Ltd (t/a Beaver International) v Barnet Football Club Ltd* (2004) 93 Con.L.R. 26, CA has confirmed: see the case at para.13–014A, above.

4. MAIN TYPES OF CONTRACT IN WHICH THE RULES HAVE BEEN DEVELOPED

(1) *Types of contract where the stipulated sum is generally a penalty*

(b) Employment contracts: failure to carry out general provisions on either side

Add at the end of the paragraph: Again in *Murray v Leisureplay plc* [2005] EWCA Civ 963, July 28, the stipulated sum was to be paid by one party — **13–048** though not as in the usual run of cases by the employee but by the employer — and in respect of one category of breach. It was held by the Court of Appeal, reversing the judge below, to be liquidated damages; facts at para.13–014D, above.

(2) *Types of contract where the stipulated sum is generally liquidated damages*

(c) Building contracts: failure to complete construction on time

13–062   NOTE 84: Insert at the beginning of the note: Also in *Alfred McAlpine Capital Projects Ltd v Tilebox Ltd* [2005] B.L.R. 271 a provision for payment at the rate of £45,000 for every week of delay in completion of building works was held to constitute liquidated damages; apart from an extended review of all the leading authorities on the subject (*ibid.*, paras 35 to 49), the lengthy judgment is taken up with attempting to assess what losses were likely to have been foreseeable at the time of contracting in order to come to a view on whether the weekly £45,000 constituted a genuine pre-estimate of loss.

5. RELATED SITUATIONS

(3) *Money which becomes payable upon some event other than breach*

(b) Obligations framed in the alternative where at least one of the alternatives is a payment of money

13–100   Add at the end of the paragraph: *Lordsvale Finance plc v Bank of Zambia* [1996] Q.B. 752, recently brought into prominence in *Murray v Leisureplay plc* [2005] EWCA Civ 963, July 28 (see at para.13–014C, above), is a modern case applying *Herbert v Salisbury & Yeovil Ry* and *General Credit Co v Clegg* (both in this para. of the main text).

BOOK ONE

PART FOUR

VARIOUS GENERAL FACTORS IN THE ASSESSMENT OF DAMAGES

CHAPTER 14

THE INCIDENCE OF TAXATION

I. INCOME TAX

(B) TYPE-SITUATIONS IN WHICH THE RULE IN GOURLEY'S *CASE MAY APPLY*

1. GENERAL CONSIDERATIONS

(1) *Mainstream* Gourley

(b) Factor (2): the damages awarded to the claimant would not themselves be subject to tax

NOTE 29: Add: The suggestion, made and rejected, in *Orthet Ltd v Vince-Cain* [2005] I.C.R. 374, EAT, that damages for injured feelings awarded in a claim under s.66(4) of the Sex Discrimination Act 1975 could be subject to tax seems very odd.

14–011

CHAPTER 15

THE AWARDING OF INTEREST

I. THE HISTORICAL LEGACY AND THE MODERN LAW

4. Overcoming the Statutory Limitations by Claiming Interest as Damages

(1) *Overcoming the limitation to simple interest*

(b) Compound interest in tort

15–017   Note 80: Add: The unsuccessful claim in *Black v Davies* [2004] EWHC 1464 (QB), June 22 to be awarded compound interest in an action of deceit was based on an attempt to harness the rule, itself still uncertain, that compound interest may be awarded in equity where there is fraud: see further at para.15–019, n.88, below.

(c) Compound interest in equity

15–019   Note 88: Add: McCombe J. in *Black v Davies* [2004] EWHC 1464 (QB), June 22, said that that day had come (*ibid.*, para.6) but his decision that compound interest could not be awarded in the case before him, which was an action in deceit, was simply on the basis that the equitable remedy of compound interest should be ancillary to an equitable cause of action. On the other hand, the Court of Appeal concluded that the authorities were to be interpreted as indeed allowing compound interest to be awarded where the obtaining of money or other benefit through fraud gave rise to an action in equity. This however did not avail the particular claimants because, whether they were still suing only in deceit or attempting to widen their attack by a claim in equity, the defendant's fraudulent representation had not caused him to obtain and retain money belonging to the claimants but had simply caused them to lose money: see [2005] EWCA Civ 531, May 6, especially at paras 87 to 89.

(d) Compound interest in arbitrations

NOTE 90: Add at the end: And see now the Law Commission's Report (at para.15–021, below) which states at para.2.45:   **15–020**

> "We understand that practice in awarding interest differs, but that compound interest is frequently awarded in large commercial and maritime claims."

A footnote (*ibid.*, note 51) adds:

> "The London Maritime Arbitrators Association told us that it was 'their general practice' to award compound interest 'quite simply because it seems commercially just to do so'. The Worshipful Company of Arbitrators commented that 'the power to award compound interest should be exercised unless there is good reason in the particular case not to do so; this, however, is noted not to be universal practice.'"

(e) Compound interest in the future

Add at the end of the paragraph: Following its Consultation Paper entitled   **15–021**
Compound Interest, the Law Commission's Report entitled *Pre-Judgment Interest on Debt and Damages* (Law Com. No.287 (2004)) has now appeared and favours, as did the Consultation Paper, the introduction of compound interest. The summary (at *ibid.*, para.1.18) of the second of its two principal recommendations (the first concerns rate of interest, for compound and simple interest alike: see para.15–087, below) runs thus:

> "The courts should have power to award compound (rather than simple) interest in appropriate circumstances. In broad terms, we think that compound interest is usually appropriate in large cases, and recommend that in payments of £15,000 or more there should be a rebuttable presumption in favour of compound interest. For payments of less than £15,000 the rebuttable presumption would be that interest is simple."

II. PARTICULAR TYPE-SITUATIONS IN WHICH INTEREST MAY BE AWARDABLE

2. TORT

(a) Torts affecting property other than land

(iii) Damage

15–042   NOTE 12: Add at the end: But they are if the claimant is impecunious: *Lagden v O'Connor* [2004] 1 A.C. 1067 at para.32–017A, below.

(c) Torts affecting the person

(i) Personal injury and wrongful death

15–053   NOTE 78: Add at the end: The Law Commission in its Report on *Pre-Judgment Interest on Debt and Damages* recommending that a general power to award compound interest should be introduced (see para.15–021, above) further, and rightly, recommends that interest on damages for non-pecuniary loss in personal injury cases should continue to be single and not compound: see Law Com. No.287 (2004) at paras 7.8 to 7.12.

III. CALCULATION OF THE AMOUNT OF INTEREST

1. PERIOD OF TIME FOR WHICH INTEREST IS AWARDED

(2) *Time from which interest runs*

(b) Interest from a time after accrual of the cause of action

15–066   NOTE 23: For para.6–030 read para.630.

(3) *Effect of delay on time to and from which interest runs*

(b) Manner in which delay affects the calculation of the interest award

15–082   NOTE 9: Add at the end: Similarly in *Hamilton-Jones v David & Snape* [2004] 1 W.L.R. 924 (solicitor's negligence).

15–083   NOTE 12: Add at the end: *Hellenic Industrial Development Bank SA v Atkin (The Julia)* [2003] Lloyd's Rep. I.R. 365 (a claim on an insurance policy): four years' interest out of the eight years from loss to judgment allowed; *Eagle v Chambers (No.2)* [2004] 1 W.L.R. 3081, CA (where no reference to interest appears in either the catchwords or the headnote to the report, so see *ibid.*, paras 99 to 101): seven years out of the 14 and a half years from injury to judgment disallowed.

(b) Periods by which interest is reduced

NOTE 14: Add at the end: *Eagle v Chambers (No.2)* [2004] 1 W.L.R. 3081, CA (at n.12, above).　　　　　**15–085**

NOTE 19: Add at the end: As much as seven years in *Eagle v Chambers (No.2)* [2004] 1 W.L.R. 3081, CA (at n.12, above).

NOTE 20: Add at the end: Buxton L.J. in *Eagle v Chambers (No.2)* [2004] 1 W.L.R. 3081, CA (at n.12, above) said that in cases where the inordinate delay was due not to the claimant — particularly where a child or a patient — but to the claimant's solicitors, the need to deprive the claimant of his full compensation might some day be reconsidered but for the present the claimant's only remedy would be an action based on negligence against his solicitors: see *ibid.*, paras 110 to 112.

2. RATE OF INTEREST

(1) *General overview: the various rates of interest*

Add at the end of the paragraph: These recommendations in its Consultation Paper follow through to the Law Commission's Report on *Pre-Judgment Interest on Debt and Damages*: see Law Com. No.287 (2004) para.1.18 and paras 10.1 and 10.2.　　　　　**15–087**

(2) *Cases in the Commercial Court and analogous cases*

(a) The developing position

NOTE 75: Add: Forbes J.'s comments about small concerns having to borrow at 3 per cent over base rate fits with the holding, 20 years later, in *Jaura v Ahmed* [2002] EWCA Civ 210, February 21: see the case at para.15–097A, below.　　　　　**15–095**

(b) The position today

Insert a new note after the first sentence of the paragraph:　　　　　**15–096**

NOTE 80a: Interest at base rate less 1 per cent was all that was awarded in *University of Keele v Price Waterhouse* [2004] P.N.L.R. 8, p.112 but that was because the claimant had conceded that this was the rate it would have earned on the moneys; see *ibid.*, paras 70 and 71. No issue on interest appears in the appeal: [2004] P.N.L.R. 43, p.888, CA.

Insert a new note after the penultimate sentence of the paragraph:

NOTE 86a: US prime rate was also held in *Hellenic Industrial Development Bank SA v Atkin (The Julia)* [2003] Lloyd's Rep. I.R. 365 to be "the appropriate rate" (*ibid.*, para.19) to award and for the same reason. Again it was a claim on an insurance policy.

Insert a new paragraph after para.15–097:

15–097A   This trend to higher rates received a boost from the decision of the Court of Appeal in *Jaura v Ahmed* [2002] EWCA Civ 210, February 21. The claimant suffered a wrongful forfeiture of the lease that he had taken of business premises. Because of reduced profits in the business he had entered into sub-leases of substantial parts of the premises in order to help service the bank overdraft which to the knowledge of his lessor, the defendant, he had incurred in order to finance the purchase. The wrongful termination deprived the claimant of the rents from the sub-leases so that he incurred a liability for accumulating interest on the overdraft. The Court of Appeal held him entitled to interest at 3 per cent over base rate to reflect the interest incurred on the overdraft. Rix L.J. who gave the only judgment on interest, with which the other two members of the court agreed, said:

> "It is right that defendants who have kept small businessmen out of money to which a court ultimately judges them to be entitled should pay a rate which properly reflects the real cost of borrowing incurred by such a class of businessmen. The law should be prepared to recognise, as I suspect evidence might well reveal, that the borrowing costs generally incurred by them are well removed from the conventional rate of 1% above base (and sometimes even less) available to first class borrowers."

This sensible decision is coming to be prayed in aid by claimants, as by the third claimant, a magazine publisher, in *Douglas v Hello! Ltd (No.7)* [2004] E.M.L.R. 14, p.230 though, on the facts there, without success: *ibid.*, at para.22. This was because the trial judge was not satisfied that the claimant had borrowed money at all, in which case the rate at which it could have invested, on which there was no evidence, would have been appropriate. In the result the judge awarded the amount claimed discounted by 20 per cent.

(c) Deviations from the commercial rate

(i) Judgment debt rate

15–100   NOTE 4: Add: Also *Hamilton-Jones v David & Snape* [2004] 1 W.L.R. 924.

(ii) Special investment account rate

Insert a new note at the end of the second sentence of the paragraph: **15–101**

NOTE 7a: But Neuberger J., without reasons, reverted to judgment debt rate in *Hamilton-Jones v David & Snape* [2004] 1 W.L.R. 924.

THE EFFECT OF CHANGES IN VALUE

3. CHANGES IN THE VALUE OF MONEY

(1) *General change in the internal value of sterling over the years*

16–012 NOTE 35: For para.35–227 read para.35–229.

(3) *Particular changes in the external value of sterling between the time of accrual of the cause of action and the time of judgment*

(c) **The working out of the *Miliangos* decision**

(ii) Contract: unliquidated damages

16–042 Add at the end of the paragraph: On the other hand, in *Virani Ltd v Manuel Revert y Cia SA* [2004] 2 Lloyd's Rep. 14, CA the currency of loss and the contemplation of the parties coincided. The claimant, an English company which had sold a quantity of cloth it had imported from Pakistan to the defendant, a Spanish company, at a price expressed in pesetas contended that the damages in its action for breach of contract on the defendant's refusing to take delivery should be expressed in US dollars; the defendant contended for euros (pesetas no longer being a currency in use), which conversion was much more favourable to it. Since the contract was of no assistance in arriving at the correct solution — that the price was expressed in pesetas was in no way controlling — the proper approach was to inquire which currency most truly expressed the claimant's loss. This was held to be US dollars, for which currency the evidence was said to be all one way. The price of the claimant's purchase from Pakistan had to be paid in dollars. Its contract price to Spain was based on its internal costings calculated in dollars. Dealing in the international market it was anxious to protect itself against fluctuations in exchange rates and it had provided itself with cover by selling forward the expected amount of pesetas in exchange for dollars. Next, it had to be established that the parties must be taken reasonably to have had a dollar currency in their contemplation, and this too was answered in the claimant's favour since the defendant, being a large dealer in cloth as familiar as was the claimant with the vagaries of rising and falling exchange rates, must have expected of anyone engaged in foreign transactions that steps would be taken to protect the value of a transaction by covering it in the way the claimant had done.

(iii) Tort

NOTE 31: For para.35–010 read para.35–210.   **16–051**

CHAPTER 17

THE RECOVERY OF COSTS, DAMAGES AND FINES INCURRED IN PREVIOUS PROCEEDINGS

II. COSTS, DAMAGES AND FINES IN PREVIOUS PROCEEDINGS BETWEEN THE NOW CLAIMANT AND THIRD PARTIES

1. THE MODERN RULE

17–017   NOTE 70: Add: And see now *Grocutt v Khan* [2003] Lloyd's Rep. I.R. 464, CA at para.17–018A, below.

Insert new paragraphs after para.17–018:

17–018A   Fortunately, the Court of Appeal has now awarded costs as damages in *Grocutt v Khan* [2003] Lloyd's Rep. I.R. 464, CA, a somewhat unusual and complex case. The claimant and the defendant doctors, when hiring a car together for an outing for themselves and their companions in the course of a medical conference which they were attending abroad, agreed contractually that the defendant would take out a comprehensive insurance policy for them against accident. An accident occurred when the claimant was driving and the defendant's mother who was injured brought a legally aided action for damages against the claimant which was dismissed with costs awarded to him. Unable to recover these costs from the mother and also from the insurance company because the defendant had lost the policy, he claimed them from the defendant as damages for breach of contract and succeeded. Lord

Phillips M.R. opened his judgment by saying that all that was at stake was the claimant's unrecovered costs in the earlier action and, while he found that the facts were unusual and raised interesting questions of legal analysis, he was "in no doubt as to the result" that flowed from the facts as found even if the precise route to that result was somewhat uncertain: *ibid.*, para.1. Costs as damages were also awarded in *Browning v Brachers* [2004] P.N.L.R. 28, p.517. An action by buyers against their seller for breach of warranty was dismissed with costs against them on account of the negligent handling of the litigation by their solicitor. In their subsequent claim against the solicitor these costs were without difficulty awarded as damages: see *ibid.*, paras 94 to 98 and the facts at para.8–055C, above. There was an appeal — [2005] EWCA Civ 753, June 20 — but this award of costs as damages was not challenged: see *ibid.*, para.149.

Yet in *Pearce v European Reinsurance Consultants and Run-Off Ltd* [2005] **17–018B** EWHC 1493 (Ch), July 12, the trial judge, not having the cases in the above paragraph cited to him, was impressed by the authorities that have moved away from the traditional position on costs as damages, though he was unprepared to come to a decision summarily on the issue: see *ibid.*, paras 22 to 30. He also referred to an unreported decision, *Yudt v Leonard Ross & Craig*, July 24, 1998, where Ferris J. felt compelled as a matter of comity to follow Carnwarth J. in the *Hextall Erskine* case (at para.17–017 of the main text) while confessing to be impressed by what he called the vigorous criticism of that decision advanced in this work (at para.17–018 of the main text). It may be that the issue will, one day soon, have to be addressed four-square by the Court of Appeal who, one trusts, will immediately appreciate that a departure from the century-old line of authority offends against the age-old principle, stemming from Lord Blackburn in *Livingstone* (at para.1–022 of the main text), that the claimant is to be put, as far as money can do it, into the same position as he would have been in had he not sustained the wrong in question.

3. MAIN TYPE-SITUATIONS IN WHICH COSTS, DAMAGES AND FINES HAVE BEEN CLAIMED AS DAMAGES

(a) Costs and damages where the now claimant has been sued

(i) Sale of goods

NOTE 80: Insert at the beginning of the note: *Contigroup Companies Inc v* **17–023** *Glencore AG* [2005] 1 Lloyd's Rep. 241 (damages and settlement);

(iv) Miscellaneous

Insert a new note in the first line of the paragraph after "Other situations": **17–027**

NOTE 91a: See too the unusual *Grocutt v Khan* [2003] Lloyd's Rep. I.R. 464, CA (at para.17–018A, above) involving an agreement to take out accident liability insurance where the action by the third party was for an accident injury.

(b) Costs where the now claimant has himself sued

(ii) Miscellaneous

17–030   NOTE 9: Add at the end: Or has sued the seller: *Browning v Brachers* [2005] EWCA Civ 753, June 20.

4. THE VARIOUS ASPECTS OF REMOTENESS OF DAMAGE INVOLVED

(2) Reasonableness of defending or bringing the previous proceedings

17–038   NOTE 45: Add at the end of the note: *Contigroup Companies Inc v Glencore AG* [2005] 1 Lloyd's Rep. 241 (delayed delivery of goods sold) is a further case where the amount paid in settlement was held to be reasonable.

(3) Causation

17–044   Add at the end of the paragraph: Lack of causation reappears in the complexities of *The Vatis T* [2004] 2 Lloyd's Rep. 465 as a ground for refusing recovery. The now defendant had time-chartered a vessel to the now claimant who sub-chartered her to the third party on a voyage charter. The now defendant claimed against the now claimant for breach of the obligation to provide a safe port and berth and in turn the now claimant claimed similarly against the third party. The now claimant counterclaimed against the now defendant for breach of the obligation of seaworthiness and the third party did likewise against the now claimant. It turned out that all had been due to the unseaworthiness of the vessel with no question of an unsafe port and berth, so that the now defendant's claim against the now claimant was discontinued and this resulted in discontinuance of the now claimant's claim against the third party. The now claimant then attempted to recover from the now defendant the costs incurred in its claim against the third party and failed because no causal link could be found between the breach by the now defendant of the obligation of seaworthiness and the now claimant's failed claim against the third party for breach of a different obligation *viz.*, the obligation to provide a safe port and berth: see *ibid.*, paras 17 and 19.

5. AMOUNT RECOVERABLE

17–055   NOTE 20: Insert after the reference to *General Feeds v Slobodna Plovidba*: and *Contigroup Companies Inc v Glencore AG* [2005] 1 Lloyd's Rep. 241.

Insert a new note at the end of the paragraph: **17–057**

NOTE 32a: See too *Browning v Brachers* [2004] P.N.L.R. 28, p.517 where the costs order had not been enforced by the time of the further claim: see the case at paras 8–055C and 17–018A, above. The award of costs as damages was not challenged on the appeal: see [2005] EWCA Civ 753, June 20, at para.149.

Insert after the third sentence of the paragraph: In *Grocutt v Khan* [2003]   **17–060** Lloyd's Rep. I.R. 464, CA (at para.17–018A, above), where again the now claimant had successfully defended, the damages were measured by the costs which he had been unable to recover because the claimant in the earlier action had been legally aided.

BOOK TWO
PARTICULAR CLAIMS

CHAPTER 19

THE MEASURE OF DAMAGES IN CONTRACT AND TORT COMPARED

NOTE 50: But certainty has been achieved, by way of a clear refusal of **19–008** recovery for mental distress, where unfair dismissal is concerned: *Dunnachie v Kingston upon Hull City Council* [2005] 1 A.C. 226 at para.3–029, above. Nothing further on mental distress and non-pecuniary loss appears in *Eastwood v Magnox Electric plc* [2005] 1 A.C. 503.

NOTE 74: Add at the end: In *Sandeman Coprimar SA v Transitos y Trans-* **19–009** *portes Integrales SL* [2003] Q.B. 1270, CA the Court of Appeal undoubtedly accepted that in a negligent conversion the test was reasonable foreseeability: see *ibid.*, paras 25 to 31. The case is considered at paras 6–184A and 6–184B, above.

NOTE 89: Add: Indeed the principle in *The Liesbosch* has now finally been **19–010** abandoned in *Lagden v O'Connor* [2004] 1 A.C. 1067: see para.6–101A, above.

BOOK TWO
PART ONE
CONTRACT

CHAPTER 20

SALE OF GOODS

I. BREACH BY SELLER

2. DELAYED DELIVERY

(2) *Consequential losses*

(b) Loss on a resale

(ii) Compensation paid to a sub-buyer

Add at the end of the paragraph: A modern case in which compensation paid **20–048**
to a sub-buyer was allowed as damages is *Contigroup Companies Inc v Glenmore
AG* [2005] 1 Lloyd's Rep. 241 where there was no available market for the buyer
to acquire equivalent goods, a sub-sale was within the contemplation of the
parties, and the compensation to the sub-buyer was by way of settlement.

3. BREACH OF CONDITION: GOODS PROPERLY REJECTED

Add at the end of the paragraph: In *Clegg v Andersson t/a Nordic Machine* **20–054**
[2003] 2 Lloyd's Rep. 32, CA, where a yacht sold was rejected by the buyer as
not of satisfactory quality because of an overweight keel, the buyer was
awarded as damages the price, other acquisition costs and consequential
losses, but no useful detail is available as the assessment of the damages was
to be referred to a Master: all at *ibid.*, paras 67 to 69.

4. BREACH OF CONDITION OR WARRANTY AS TO QUALITY, FITNESS OR DESCRIPTION: GOODS ACCEPTED

(1) *Normal measure*

20–057   NOTE 39: Add at the end: Since in *Bramhill v Edwards* [2004] 2 Lloyd's Rep. 653, CA the buyers of a motor home had not proved that its width marginally in excess of the permitted width had any effect on its value, their damages claim could not succeed.

(2) *Consequential losses*

(b) Loss through use and through loss of use

(i) Loss of user profits

20–071   NOTE 89: Add at the end: A further unsuccessful claim is *Filobake Ltd v Rondo Ltd* [2005] EWCA Civ 563, May 11 (at para.2–039A, above).

5. BREACH OF CONDITION AS TO TITLE OR OF WARRANTY OF QUIET POSSESSION

20–100   Add at the end of the paragraph: *Louis Dreyfus Trading Ltd v Reliance Trading Ltd* [2004] 2 Lloyd's Rep. 243, provides an illustration of damages for breach of the warranty of quiet possession where the damages were necessarily different from those in *Mason v Burningham* (in this paragraph in the main text) since here the buyer had eventually obtained possession of the goods sold, in this case a cargo of sugar. Discharge of the cargo from the vessel upon which it was being shipped was delayed by reason of an injunction restraining discharge obtained by a third party — it was this that gave rise to the breach of the warranty of quiet possession — and when the injunction was finally lifted and the claimant received the sugar, its price in the market had fallen. The *prima facie* measure of damages, which arbitrators awarded, was held to be, using the analogy of damages for breach of warranty of quality, the difference between the contract price and the value of the sugar when it was eventually received. On the appeal this as the correct *prima facie* measure was not challenged (though, strictly, it should have been phrased as the difference between the value as warranted and the value received, which may well have given the same result), but there was an issue as to whether this was an appropriate measure in the light of a sub-sale which had been made by the claimant before it had contracted with the defendant; this issue is dealt with at para.6–166, above.

II. BREACH BY BUYER

1. NON-ACCEPTANCE

(1) *Normal measure*

(b) Relevant and irrelevant prices in ascertaining the market price

NOTE 94: Add at the end: The price for which the seller sold a business to **20–111** the buyer, where the breach was however not by the buyer but by the solicitor advising on the sale, was held not to be relevant to the assessment of damages in *Matlaszek v Bloom Camillin* [2004] P.N.L.R. 17, p.309; see *ibid.*, paras 6 and 7, and the case at para.29–009, n.35, below.

SALE OF LAND

II. BREACH BY BUYER

(B) BREACH OF COVENANTS

2. RESTRICTIVE COVENANTS

22–053   Add a new note at the end of the paragraph:

NOTE 13a: Damages for a buyer's breach of a covenant not to build also featured in *Harris v Williams-Wynne* [2005] EWHC 151 (Ch), February 11.

Insert new paragraphs after para.22–053:

22–053A   *Lane v O'Brien Homes* [2004] EWHC 303 (QB), February 5, is a further illustration of a claim by a seller of land against his buyer concerned with overbuilding, in this case building a fourth house on the land when the buyer had agreed to build only three. The case differs from the general run in two respects. First, the building had not been built by the time of the litigation; only planning permission for it had been applied for and had been granted. Secondly, the breach was of a collateral contract and not of a covenant in the sale contract itself. The defendant buyer argued, on the strength of the recovery allowed in *Wrotham Park* (at para.22–050 of the main text), that he should be liable for only 5 per cent of the profit to be made on the fourth house, the claimant argued that he was entitled to the whole of the profit on the fourth house, and the trial judge awarded in the region of half of this profit. However, in arriving at this result he entered, unnecessarily, the lists of loss of a chance doctrine, saying that the court must assess the degree of probability that the benefit lost as a result of the breach of contract would accrue to the claimant. But all that was needed was to assess the percentage of the profit which should in fairness accrue to the claimant, and this was indeed accepted on the appeal in *Lane*: see *ibid.*, para.22.

The appeal in *Lane* dealt also with the time at which the percentage of the **22–053B** profit to be paid over in damages fell to be assessed. When the contract of sale was entered into, the prospect of obtaining planning permission for a fourth house was not thought promising by either contracting party so that at that time the defendant would have had to pay a good deal less than half of his notional profit to the claimant for his permission. However the appeal judge, in upholding the trial judge's award, said at *ibid.*, para.25 that he was

> "satisfied that the *Wrotham Park* principle requires the court to con-
> sider the course of hypothetical negotiations for the release from the
> prohibition not at the time of the sale, but later".

The later time chosen as the relevant time was the time the defendant would have sought release from his contractual commitment, namely, when plan-ning permission had been granted. And with planning permission a certainty "the stakes had become very much higher": *ibid.*, para.25. It could of course be said that, if the damages are still to be regarded as compensation for loss of a bargaining opportunity, then for the purposes of an assessment of the damages one should look to the time of contracting, which is when the bar-gaining would have taken place. If however one regards the damages award, as one today should, as one of restitutionary damages, there is no difficulty in basing the damages on the profit that the defendant is going to make: see paras 12–022 to 12–023, above and Ch.12 generally.

LEASE OF LAND

I. BREACH BY LESSOR

(C) BREACH OF COVENANTS

1. COVENANT FOR QUIET ENJOYMENT AND COVENANT AGAINST INCUMBRANCES

(1) *Total eviction*

23–015   Add at the end of the paragraph: In *Jaura v Ahmed* [2002] EWCA 210, February 21, the facts of which are at para.15–097A, above, it was recognised that the normal measure of damages for wrongful eviction is the value of the unexpired term calculated by rental value less contractual rent (*ibid.*, para.9) and the recovery there for the loss of anticipated profit rental from sub-lettings but not, as duplication, for the capital value of the lease may be said to represent an application of this normal measure.

23–016   Add at the end of the paragraph: In *Jaura v Ahmed* [2002] EWCA 210, February 21, the facts of which are at para.15–097A, above, the expenditure on fixtures and fittings which remained on the premises and were thus lost to the lessee on account of the eviction, and for which recovery was allowed, could be regarded as a consequential loss.

2. Covenant to Repair

(1) *Normal measure*

Insert a new note after the colon on the third line of the paragraph: **23–023**

Note 78a: The curious case of *Bluestorm Ltd v Portvale Holdings Ltd* [2004] H.L.R. 49, p.939, CA shows not only that the lessor will not be liable on its repairing covenant where the lessee's breach causes the lessor to be unable to effect the repairs but also that any loss thereby caused to the lessor is recoverable from the lessee.

(3) *Non-pecuniary loss*

Note 24 Add at the end: Also in *Shine v English Churches Housing Group* **23–030** [2004] H.LR. 42, p.727, CA failure to mitigate reduced the award: see the case at para.7–043, above.

Add at the end of the paragraph: *Wallace* was stated by the Court of **23–031** Appeal in *Shine v English Churches Housing Group* [2004] H.L.R. 42, p.727, CA to be "plainly the leading case" on awards for discomfort and inconvenience in this context: see *ibid.*, para.94. In *Shine* the court purported to follow the guidelines set out in *Wallace* and, of the three methods of assessment set out there by Morritt L.J., that based upon a notional reduction of the rent was followed. While the court accepted that "there will be cases in which the level of distress or inconvenience experienced by a tenant may require an award in excess of the level of rental payable" (*ibid.*, para.104) this was not such a case and, since the trial judge had awarded an amount well beyond the rental figure, his award was very substantially reduced, from £19,000 to £8,000. The court also explained why they considered it proper to have regard to financial considerations in arriving at damages for non-financial loss by saying that it was "in our judgment logical that the calculation of the award of damages for stress and inconvenience should be related to the fact that the tenant is not getting proper value for the rent, which is being paid for defective premises" (*ibid.*, para.105). This approach is borne out by the further Court of Appeal decision in *Niazi Services Ltd v Van der Loo* [2004] H.L.R. 34, p.562, CA where the method of assessment by a notional reduction of the rent payable was again used in the assessment of the damages: see *ibid.*, paras 27 to 30. Since the breaches of covenant to repair were on a comparatively small scale, of a much less serious nature than in *Shine*, the defendants argued for a smallish sum but because the property was a high-class flat in a very high-class neighbourhood with a high rent — £34,800 per annum as compared with the £2,600 per annum in *Shine* — the tenant was paying for and entitled to expect high-class standards, and this argument was rejected: see *ibid.*, at para.31.

II. BREACH BY LESSEE

(B) BREACH OF COVENANTS

1. COVENANT TO REPAIR

23–043   NOTE 64: Add at the end: And the lessee's repair of the roof was held to be adequate without requiring its complete replacement, which had been effected by the lessor on the lease's termination, in *Riverside Property Investments Ltd v Blackhawk Automotive* [2005] 1 E.G.L.R. 114.

(3) *Measure of damages in action at determination of tenancy*

(b) As limited by statute: post-1927

23–057   NOTE 48: Add at the end: Again in *Mason v Totalfinaelf UK Ltd* [2003] 3 E.G.L.R. 91 there was a finding of cost of repair as well as of diminution in value, and with a substantial difference between the two; the repair cost for a petrol filling station of £134,738 was nearly double the diminution in value of £73,500.

3. COVENANT AGAINST ASSIGNMENT OR UNDERLETTING

Insert a new paragraph after para.23–094:

23–094A   An entirely different type of claim by a lessor for breach of the covenant not to underlet has appeared in *Crestfort Ltd v Tesco Stores Ltd* [2005] EWHC 805 (Ch), May 25, being a claim for compensatory damages in the amount that the lessor would have demanded for relaxing the covenant against underletting. This is analogous to the many more authorities, at paras 22–049 to 22–053 of the main text, dealing with claims by a seller of land where covenants against building have been breached by the buyer. See the case at *ibid.*, para.72 *et seq.*

CHAPTER 24

SALE OF SHARES AND LOAN OF STOCK

II. BREACH BY BUYER

1. NON-ACCEPTANCE

NOTE 30: Add at the end: The price for which the seller sold shares to the **24–009** buyer, where the breach was however not by the buyer but by the solicitor advising on the sale, was held not to be relevant to the assessment of damages in *Matlaszek v Bloom Camillin* [2004] P.N.L.R. 17, p.309; see *ibid.*, paras 6 and 7, and the case at para.29–009, n.35, below.

CHAPTER 25

CONTRACTS TO PAY OR TO LEND MONEY

I. BREACH BY PARTY PROMISING TO PAY

2. Dishonour of Bills of Exchange and Promissory Notes

(2) *Bills and notes to which section 57 applies*

(b) Interest

(ii) Period of time for which interest is given

25–016   NOTE 94: For para.15–008 read para.15–088.

CHAPTER 26

BUILDING CONTRACTS

NOTE 7: Add at the end: See also *Johnson Control Systems Ltd v Techni-* **26–002**
Track Europa Ltd (2003) 91 Con.L.R. 88, CA, which concerned a dispute
between a sub-contractor and a sub-sub-contractor on a construction project, the one having sub-contracted part of the work to the other. The details
on the damages are very confusing.

I. BREACH BY BUILDER

2. DELAY IN COMPLETING BUILDING

Insert a new paragraph after para.26–008:

Delay does make an appearance in a damages context in *Earl's Terrace* **26–008A**
Properties Ltd v Nilsson Design Ltd [2004] B.L.R. 273 though the claim made
was against the architect rather than the builder. The claimants were devel-
opers who were refurbishing on a grand scale a row of London terrace
houses. Their architect's inadequate design resulted in faulty installations
which required remedial work delaying the completion of the houses and
their handover to the claimants for sale by 15 months. This caused delay in
the return to the claimants of their capital locked into the project (*ibid.*,
para.72) and they successfully claimed for their loss on account of their funds
being held within the development project and not released by the selling of
the houses.

3. DEFECTIVE BUILDING

(1) *Normal measure*

26–013   Add at the end of the paragraph: In *Birse Construction Ltd v Eastern Tele-graph Company Ltd* [2004] EWHC 2512 (TCC), November 5, where a residential training college was built with defects by the defendant construction company for the claimants who intended to sell the college, there could be no recovery of the cost of remedying defects which the claimants were not proposing to remedy before they sold: see *ibid.*, at paras 51 to 54.

CONTRACTS OF CARRIAGE

I. BREACH BY CARRIER

(A) CARRIAGE OF GOODS

1. NON-DELIVERY INCLUDING DELIVERY IN A DAMAGED CONDITION

NOTE 5: Add at the end: For an unusual case of loss through loss in tran-   **27–002**
sit arising in the context of a contract of carriage of goods see *Sandeman
Coprimar SA v Transitos y Transportes Integrales SL* [2003] Q.B. 1270, CA at
paras 6–184A and 6–184B, above.

(2) *Consequential losses*

Add a new note at the end of the paragraph: **27–012**

NOTE 52a: For an unusual consequential loss arising in the context of a
contract of carriage of goods see *Sandeman Coprimar SA v Transitos y
Transportes Integrales SL* [2003] Q.B. 1270, CA at paras 6–184A and 6–184B,
above.

II. BREACH BY CARGO OWNER

27–060   NOTE 47: Add at the end: See *Odfjell Seachem A/S v Continentale des Petroles et d'Investissements* [2005] 1 Lloyd's Rep. 275 for a further decision on damages, involving repudiation of a charterparty and a claim by the owners for their lost profit, including demurrage at beginning and end, and taking into account a substitute charter entered into in mitigation.

1. FAILURE TO SUPPLY CARGO

(1) *Normal measure*

(b) Circumstances in which substitute freight which has or could have been earned is not deducted

27–071   NOTE 97: Add at the end: For similar reasons in *The Golden Victory* [2005] 1 Lloyd's Rep. 443 the normal measure of market freight less substitute freight was held recoverable for only part of the contractual period that remained after the accepted repudiatory breach: facts at para.8–062, n.48, above.

THOMSON

™

SWEET & MAXWELL

Thank you for purchasing **McGregor on Damages, 2nd supplement to the 17th edition.**

Supplements to your main work

McGregor is supplemented regularly in order to keep your main work up-to-date with ongoing developments.

In order to receive your updating supplements to **McGregor** automatically on publication *you need to register*. Supplements will be invoiced on publication. You can cancel your request at any time.

How to register

Either complete and return this FREEPOST card, or, if you have purchased your copy of **McGregor** from a bookshop or other supplier, please ask your supplier to ensure that you are registered to receive your supplements.

Yes, please send me updating supplements to **McGregor on Damages, 17th edition** on publication, unless countermanded.

Name: _____

Organisation: _____

_____

Address: _____

_____

_____

Postcode: _____

Telephone: _____

Email: _____

S&M account number: (if known) _____

Signed: _____ Date: _____

LBU0975I

STANDING ORDERS
SWEET & MAXWELL
FREEPOST
PO Box 2000
ANDOVER
SP10 9AH
UNITED KINGDOM

CONTRACTS OF EMPLOYMENT

I. BREACH BY EMPLOYER

1. WRONGFUL DISMISSAL

NOTE 1: Insert after the reference to *Wilding v British Telecommunications* **28–001**
plc in the middle of the note: However, there is currently some disagreement
in the Employment Appeal Tribunal as to whether mitigation principles do
apply to the compensation for loss of earnings which are awarded for the
notice period to which an unfairly dismissed employee is entitled. *Hardy v
Polk (Leeds) Ltd* [2004] I.R.L.R. 420 held that they did apply, requiring the
deduction of earnings in other employment taken during the notice period,
with *Voith Turbo Ltd v Stowe* [2005] I.C.R. 543 later disagreeing and making
no such deduction.

Insert after the reference to *H.M. Prison Service v Salmon* towards the end
of the note: In discrimination cases the statutory compensation is to follow
the principles applicable to tort damages claims: *Atos Origin IT Services UK
Ltd v Haddock* [2005] I.C.R. 277.

Add at the end of the note: It was held in *Kingston upon Hull City Council
v Dunnachie (No.3)* [2004] I.C.R. 227 that, while the Ogden Tables have been
prepared for use in personal injury and fatal accident cases (see the Tables at
para.35–054 of the main text), they may be used in employment tribunal
cases but that their use should be rare and confined to calculations of career-
long losses.

(1) *Normal measure*

(a) The amount the employee would have earned under the contract

28–003   NOTE 4: Insert after the reference to *Lavarack v Woods of Colchester*: and *Horkulak v Cantor Fitzgerald International* [2005] I.C.R. 402, CA.

28–005   Insert a new note at the end of the second sentence of the paragraph:

NOTE 21a: There was an unsuccessful attempt to carry it too far in *Harper v Virgin Net Ltd* [2004] I.R.L.R. 390, CA by claiming, in the employee's action for damages for wrongful dismissal, for the loss of a chance of recovering compensation for unfair dismissal: see the case at para.8–052, n.12, above.

Insert new paragraphs after para.28–007:

28–007A   At first instance in *Horkulak v Cantor Fitzgerald International* [2003] I.C.R. 697 *Lavarack* was distinguished since in *Horkulak* the claimant employee had the benefit of a term in his contract which entitled him to receive a discretionary bonus: see *ibid.*, paras 85 and 86. On the appeal, [2005] I.C.R. 402, CA, the Court of Appeal agreed that the *ratio* of *Lavarack* was not decisive of the case, *Lavarack* not being concerned with the true construction of a discretionary bonus clause: see *ibid.*, paras 31 to 36. The issue for the trial judge was therefore whether, in line with the employer defendant's obligation to exercise its discretion reasonably and in good faith, the discretionary bonus would have been paid, and he held that it would have been: see [2003] I.C.R. 697, paras 86 and 89 *et seq.* The Court of Appeal was of the view that the judge was correct to hold that the claimant would have been entitled, had he remained in the employment, to a bona fide and rational exercise by his employers of their discretion and further that the judge's holding that the discretion would have been exercised in his favour had not been shown to be wrong: see [2005] I.C.R. 402, CA, paras 46 and 50.

28–007B   There then remained the question of the level of bonus that would have been paid. The Court of Appeal examined the judge's approach to this vital question in the utmost detail (*ibid.*, paras 60 to 92) and, while not upholding any of the criticisms of it put forward by the employer, took the view that the judge had not explained his reasons adequately for arriving at his bonus figures and sent the matter back to him for further consideration and elucidation (*ibid.*, paras 93 and 105). Of particular importance in this connection is the Court of Appeal's dealing with the relationship between the rule that a defendant is entitled to perform the contract in the least onerous manner and the rule that the freedom of choice of method of performance is limited by reasonableness, issues which are fully considered, together with the cases of *Paula Lee* and *Lion Nathan* adverted to by the Court of Appeal, at paras 8–060 to 8–064 of the main text.

For another aspect of the damages in *Horkulak*, one that was only before the trial judge, see para.8–060, above.

28–007C

NOTE 49: For para.35–112 read para.35–122.

28–010

NOTE 62: For para.32–200 read para.35–194.

NOTE 68: For para.35–152 read para.35–151.

(b) The amount the employee has or should have earned in alternative employment

Insert a new note after the fourth sentence of the paragraph:

28–013

NOTE 81a: The Court of Appeal reduced the judge's award in *Horkulak v Cantor Fitzgerald International* [2005] I.C.R. 402, CA (at para.28–007A, above) by two months' salary because of the employee's dilatoriness in taking up alternative employment: see *ibid.,* paras 95 to 101.

(2) Consequential losses

(b) The particular case of injured feelings or reputation

Add a new note at the end of the paragraph:

28–016

NOTE 1a: After having "cast a long shadow over the common law", as it was put by Lord Nicholls in *Eastwood v Magnox Electric plc* [2005] 1 A.C. 503, para.1.

(ii) Injury to reputation

NOTE 28: Add: *Addis* was again considered to stand in the way of recovery in *Disney v France Luxury Group SA* [2004] EWHC 2303 (QB), October 20.

28–019

Add at the end of the penultimate sentence of the paragraph: However, the House of Lords has held further, in *Eastwood v Magnox Electric plc* [2005] 1 A.C. 503, that, if before his unfair dismissal an employee has acquired a cause of action against his employer for breach of the obligation of trust and confidence which can be said to exist independently of the dismissal, he can bring an action for consequent financial loss and the action is not barred by the availability of a claim under the unfair dismissal legislation.

28–021   Add at the end of the paragraph: Nothing further on mental distress and non-financial loss appears in the House of Lords in *Eastwood v Magnox Electric plc* [2005] 1 A.C. 503: see the case in paragraph preceding this. Recovery for non-financial loss however has been firmly outlawed by the House in unfair dismissal claims in *Dunnachie v Kingston upon Hull City Council* [2005] 1 A.C. 226: see the case at para.3–029, above.

(iii) Loss of publicity

28–022   NOTE 43: Add at the end: Nor is a fashion designer within the category: *Disney v France Luxury Group SA* [2004] EWHC 2303 (QB), October 20; nor a theatrical production company: *Brighton v Jones* [2004] E.M.L.R. 26, p.507 (not a contract of employment; see the case at para.2–028, n.76, above).

NOTE 49: Add at the end: Contract of apprenticeship is, however, strictly construed for these damages purposes; thus there was held to be none such in *Flett v Matheson* [2005] I.C.R. 1134, EAT; see *ibid.*, para.19.

2. BREACH OF OBLIGATION OF TRUST AND CONFIDENCE

28–023   Add at the end of the paragraph: Breach of the implied term of trust and confidence was in issue at first instance in the damages claim in *Horkulak v Cantor Fitzgerald International* [2003] I.C.R. 697 but makes little or no appearance on the appeal: [2005] I.C.R. 402, CA. For the damages see the case at paras 8–060 and 28–007A to 28–007B, above.

28–024   Insert after the first sentence of the paragraph: The decision in *Mahmud* is taken further in *Eastwood v Magnox Electric plc* [2005] 1 A.C. 503: see the case at para.28–019, above.

Insert after the second sentence of the paragraph: But the discussion was not continued in *Eastwood v Magnox Electric plc* [2005] 1 A.C. 503; see para.28–019, above.

4. MISCELLANEOUS BREACHES

28–026   Insert a new note at the end of the paragraph:

NOTE 66a: A discretionary bonus was also in issue in *Horkulak v Cantor Fitzgerald International* [2005] I.C.R. 402, CA: see the case at paras 28–007A and 28–007B, above.

CHAPTER 29

CONTRACTS FOR PROFESSIONAL AND OTHER SERVICES

I. BREACH BY THE PARTY ENGAGING THE SERVICES

29–002 NOTE 5: Add at the end: Similar is *Sadler v Reynolds* [2005] EWHC 309 (QB), March 7, where the claimant had contracted with the defendant to write the defendant's autobiography but was unable to do so as the defendant in breach of contract had agreed with another to write it; he received a modest amount in damages for the loss of the opportunity to enhance his reputation. Compare the position where the contract is one of employment, at para.28–021, above and in the main text.

II. BREACH BY THE PARTY RENDERING THE SERVICES

(A) IN GENERAL

29–004 Insert a new note at the end of the paragraph:

NOTE 8a: There is of course the professionally negligent defendant, such as the barrister, who is not in contractual relations with the claimant and who therefore falls outside this chapter. Claims against barristers with damages issues therefore only make an appearance in the chapters dealing with general principles: see *Green v Alexander Johnson* [2005] EWCA Civ 775, June 28, at para.6–124, n.54, above (cause and scope of duty), *Luke v Wansbroughs* [2005] P.N.L.R. 2, p.15 at para.8–049A, above (loss of earning capacity and loss of a chance) and *Gascoine v Ian Sheridan & Co and Latham* (1994) 5 Med. L.R. 437 at para.8–045 of the main text (loss of a chance).

29–005   NOTE 16: Add: Also *University of Keele v Price Waterhouse* [2004] P.N.L.R. 8, p.112 (lost chance of implementing tax-saving scheme; facts at para.8–045, above) (damages not appealed: [2004] P.N.L.R. 43, p.888, CA); *Slattery v Moore Stephens* [2004] P.N.L.R. 14, p.241 (failure to advise, leading to unnecessary tax liability); *BE Studios Ltd v Smith & Williamson Ltd* [2005] EWHC 1506 (Ch), July 15 (failure to advise of the availability of tax relief, but no loss proved).

NOTE 18: Add at the end: *Earl's Terrace Properties Ltd v Nilsson Design Ltd* [2004] B.L.R. 273 was a claim against an architect for inadequate design (at para.26–008A, above).

Add at the end of the paragraph: The claim in *Thomson v Christie Manson & Woods Ltd* [2004] P.N.L.R. 42, p.823 was against auctioneers who had negligently misdescribed an auction lot comprising a pair of vases. But for the misdescription the claimant would not have bid for and purchased the vases. Damages fell to be assessed at the difference between the price paid, including buyer's premium, and the vases' actual worth. It would appear that the judge would have been prepared to follow *Naughton v O'Callaghan* [1990] 3 All E.R. 191 (at para.41–049 of the main text) had it been the case that the vases had depreciated in value between the date of the auction and the date when the claimant became apprised of the misdescription but he took the view that the value had not altered significantly between these two dates. Damages are not dealt with until paras 200 to 204 of the judgment. The Court of Appeal, in allowing the auctioneers' appeal on liability, said nothing about damages: [2005] EWCA Civ 555, May 12.

(B) PARTICULAR CATEGORIES

1. SOLICITORS

(1) *Pecuniary loss*

(b) Negligence in the acquisition of property by purchase

29–009   NOTE 35: Add at the end: *Matlaszek v Bloom Camillin* [2004] P.N.L.R. 17, p.309 is a useful case of a solicitor negligently failing to advise of the risks to the sellers of a company business of relying on the credit of the purchaser and the guarantor, the damages being assessed as the value of the company with which the sellers would not have parted had they been properly advised. In coming to a value the net asset basis was rejected in favour of average annual earnings multiplied by an appropriate price earnings ratio.

Insert new paragraphs after para.29–017:

A similar result to that in *Havenledge* (in the main text at para.29–017) was **29–017A**
reached in *Keydon Estate Ltd v Eversheds LLP* [2005] EWHC 972 (Ch), May
20. The claimant, a small commercial investment company, was minded to
acquire the freehold reversion of an office building with the object, known to
its solicitors who were the defendants, of obtaining a source of income by
way of rents from the lessee of the property, a substantial tenant. However,
the lessee had created a sub-lease and the claimant wished to be assured that
the lessee would nonetheless remain liable on the covenants in the lease. The
defendants' assurance that this would be so was negligent since the sub-lease
had operated as an assignment releasing the lessee as assignee from liability
on the covenants. The sub-lessee soon after went into administration, the lessee refused to pay the rents, and the claimant's income stream dried up. The
trial judge concluded that, had the claimant been correctly advised, it would
not have proceeded with the purchase but would have spent the money
thereby released in acquiring an equivalent property generating a similar
rental income stream, there being held to be other such properties available
on the market. It was emphasised that the loss for which the damages were to
be awarded was not the anticipated loss of the income stream from the freehold reversion bought but the loss of a similar stream from the alternative
property that would have been bought in the absence of the defendants' negligent advice (*ibid.*, para.31). Accordingly, the claimant's damages amounted
to the difference between the position it would have been in had it bought an
alternative property and its current position, between the likely result of such
a purchase and what in fact had transpired (*ibid.*, para.30).

In *Powell v Whitman Breed Abbot & Morgan* [2005] P.N.L.R.1, p.1 the **29–017B**
defendant solicitors, acting for the claimant in the purchase of the leasehold
of a town house which the claimant planned to renovate and resell profitably,
were asked to advise her whether it would impede the resale of the house if
she took the leasehold interest not in her own name but in that of a company.
Their advice was held to be wrong in that it would take considerably longer
to sell a company lease than an individual lease. After considering at length
a myriad of figures and calculations submitted by the parties directed at
ascertaining the proper measure of damages (*ibid.*, paras 36 to 58), the trial
judge eventually held that the award should amount to 6 per cent of the value
at the time of the claimant's purchase as a rough estimate of the loss by having the resale delayed (*ibid.*, paras 59 and 60). It is however for consideration
whether, for this calculation, the value should be rather at the date when the
resale would have taken place had the lease been in the claimant's own name.

29–017C   *Greymalkin Ltd v Copleys* [2004] P.N.L.R. 44, p.901 involved the purchase of a property where the solicitor had been negligent in failing to discover that the property was encumbered but the judgment in the case is found to be somewhat convoluted and not particularly helpful on the damages issues. The purchase was by a property development company of a decrepit hotel with the intention of converting it into flats but, because the property was subject to charges not overreached by the sale and thus creating a cloud on the title, charges which the defendant solicitor had negligently failed to uncover, the planned conversion could not come to fruition. The claimant, after spending substantial sums in preserving and repairing the property, eventually sold it at a substantial loss and claimed, under a whole series of heads, an amount in excess of half a million pounds. In this milieu the trial judge set out the principles of damages which he purported to apply in somewhat confusing detail, after having set out, also in detail, the complex rival contentions of claimant and defendant on damages, and then sought to apply these principles so as to end up with awarding what he called the *prima facie* measure of damages, which he stated as the difference at the time of purchase between the property's value without, and its value with, the cloud on title, and which amounted to under £50,000, on the basis that "there is no alternative basis of assessment that can do justice in this case" (*ibid.* para.86). He was undoubtedly right to reject most of the myriad and dubious heads of loss put forward by the claimant (see *ibid.*, para.98); and in particular to hold that the case was not a suitable one for awarding either the costs of remedying the defects as the charges clouding the title had been met, by the insurers of another solicitor, without any cost to the claimant, or the costs of extrication as the ultimate sale of the property was not effected by way of extrication from the situation in which the claimant found itself (see *ibid.*, para.86). But it is difficult to see why a claim for the claimant's wasted expenditure, subject here to the problems of proof, up until the time of knowledge of the cloud on title should not have been allowed. Moreover, what does not appear to have been noticed is that, as the claimant had bought at a price which was nearly twice the market value of the property with an unencumbered title and as the judge held that the claimant would not have bought at all had the cloud on title been revealed by the defendant (see *ibid.*, para.85), the true measure of damages that could be claimed was this purchase price less the value with the cloud on title (for this see paras 29–010 and 29–011 of the main text), a much higher sum, at over £150,000, than was awarded to the claimant. No such point appears to have been taken on the appeal, which was dismissed: [2005] P.N.L.R. 20, p.334, CA.

(e) Negligent conduct of litigation

29–024   NOTE 5: Add at the end: Also settlement at alleged undervalue: *Luke v Wansbroughs* [2005] P.N.L.R. 2, p.15 (facts at para.8–049A, above).

Add at the end of the paragraph: In *Maden v Clifford Coppock & Carter* [2005] P.N.L.R. 7, p.112, CA the solicitor's negligence consisted in giving the wrong advice to his client on the costs consequences of a claim being brought against the client with the result that the client fought the case unsuccessfully whereas, with the right costs advice, he would have settled on favourable terms. The damages were based on the difference between the client's position after the unsuccessful outcome of the litigation and his position as it would have been had he settled, although subject to discounting the award for the possibility that the settlement might not have come about. For the discount aspect of the case see para.8–042, above.

Add at the end of the paragraph: However this approach in *Charles v Hugh*   **29–025** *Jenkins & Jones* [2000] 1 W.L.R. 1278, CA has been roundly, and rightly, criticised in Scotland at first instance in *Campbell v Imray* [2004] P.N.L.R. 1, p.1, a similar case of solicitor's negligence. Lord Emslie's cogent comments are reproduced at para.8–057, above, which see.

(g) Miscellaneous

Add at the end of the paragraph: *Ball v Druces & Attlee (No.2)* [2004]   **29–031** P.N.L.R. 39, p.745 is a difficult and complex case where negligent advice of solicitors combined with loss of a chance again reappear. The claimant had retained the defendants to safeguard his interests in a project of which he was an originator and which became enormously successful. He successfully sued the defendants for negligence in allowing the project to be set up as a charitable trust, thereby preventing him from claiming any right to share in the profits generated by the project. Here there were very many acts of third parties that had to be performed before those profits would have come the claimant's way: see them set out in the judgment at paras 201 and 202. Nelson J. held that, in assessing the damages where there are various outcomes, "the right approach is to evaluate the chance of success of each of the possible outcomes, giving a percentage assessment for each category of lost chance": *ibid.*, para.275. While then it is no doubt true that the different chances lost have to be amalgamated, Nelson J. appears to have allowed recovery in respect of outcomes which should have been regarded as alternative rather than cumulative: see his conclusions on *quantum* at paras 309 to 311 and para.313.

(2) *Non-pecuniary loss*

Insert a new note after the first sentence of the paragraph: **29–033**

NOTE 56a: General damages have been awarded against solicitors for wrongful bankruptcy: *Fraser v Gaskell* [2004] P.N.L.R. 32, p.613.

Add at the end of the paragraph: *Hamilton-Jones v David & Snape* [2004] 1 W.L.R. 924 is a further case of recovery against a solicitor for non-pecuniary loss. The claimant, suing her solicitor for negligence in allowing her children to be removed to Tunisia by their Tunisian father, was held entitled to damages for the distress from being deprived of the company of, and the ability to bring up, her children and from knowing that they would be brought up in a culturally and linguistically different foreign country. While no tortious liability exists in respect of the loss of the custody and society of children, damages are nevertheless recoverable for breach of contract provided that one of the objects of the contract is to provide peace of mind. The claimant feared that the children's father would attempt to spirit them out of the country and had instructed the defendant to take the necessary steps, which he failed to do, specifically to ensure that the father would be unable to do so; thus part of the reason for the contract was to protect the claimant's peace of mind. Neuberger J. conducted a careful review of the relevant authorities: see *ibid.*, paras 43 to 64. He also considered a whole variety of factors in arriving at the figure of £20,000 for the non-pecuniary loss: see *ibid.*, paras 66 to 69.

2. SURVEYORS AND VALUERS

29–034   NOTE 67: Add at the end: For a case where the negligence consisted in a failure to make enquiries as to the likelihood of residential development of land being permitted see *Francis v Barclays Bank plc* [2005] P.N.L.R. 18, p.297 (at para.8–045, above).

(1) *Purchasers of property negligently surveyed or valued*

(a) Pecuniary loss: normal measure

29–036   Insert a new note at the end of the paragraph:

NOTE 83a: It was common ground in *McKinnon v e.surv Ltd* [2003] 2 E.G.L.R. 57 that the purchaser was entitled to the difference between the purchase price and the value of the property at the date of the purchasing valuation and the oddity of the case lay in the fact that the suspected defect did not exist although this could not have been known at the time of valuation. For how this affected the damages see the case at para.7–097, above.

(c) Non-pecuniary loss

29–045   NOTE 37: Add at the end: Contrast *Dennis v Ministry of Defence* [2003] 2 E.G.L.R. 121 at para.34–018A, below.

29–046   NOTE 41: Add at the end: And has now finally been overturned in *Lagden v O'Connor* [2004] 1 A.C. 1067: see para.6–101A, above.

Insert a new heading and a new paragraph after para. 29–063:

(3) *Vendors of property negligently surveyed or valued*

The same principles apply where too low a valuation is provided by the sur- **29–063A**
veyor or valuer to one about to sell as apply where too high a valuation is
given to an intending buyer (as in the cases at para.29–035 *et seq.* of the main
text). *Montlake v Lambert Smith Hampton Group* [2004] 3 E.G.L.R. 149 concerned the disposal by a well-known football club, Wasps, of its ground,
together with its team and its goodwill, in an arrangement whereby it
acquired shares. For the purposes of this disposal the ground was valued by
the defendants at under £1 million. This was a negligent valuation because
the defendants had failed to make proper enquiries as to the prospects of
obtaining residential planning permission. The ground was eventually sold
for £11.9 million once planning permission for residential development had
been obtained. A proper valuation by the defendants at the time of the disposal by Wasps would have produced a valuation of £3.25 million, and the
damages were based on the difference between this figure and the actual disposal figure of under £1 million. It was held not to be appropriate to base the
damages on the much higher figure at which the ground had ultimately sold
as the trial judge considered it to be improbable that Wasps, if properly
advised, would have decided to go it alone by keeping the ground out of its
disposal and taking the chance of itself obtaining the planning permission:
see *ibid.*, paras 205 to 211.

5. ESTATE AGENTS

Add at the end of the paragraph: In *John D. Wood & Co (Residential and* **29–070**
Agricultural) v Knatchbull [2003] 1 E.G.L.R. 33 the damages awarded against
the estate agent were for loss of a chance: see the case at para.8–045, above.

CHAPTER 31

CONTRACTS OF WARRANTY OF AUTHORITY BY AGENT

2. WARRANTY OF AUTHORITY TO CONTRACT ON THE PRINCIPAL'S BEHALF

(1) *The amount that would have been recoverable from the alleged principal*

31–004   NOTE 10: Add at the end: Insolvency arises again in *Skylight Maritime SA v Ascot Underwriting Ltd* [2005] P.N.L.R. 25, p.450 where the warranty was of authority to conduct litigation. See the case at para.31–017, below.

31–009   NOTE 36a: *Habton Farms v Nimmo* is now reported at [2004] Q.B. 1, CA.

3. OTHER WARRANTIES OF AUTHORITY BY AN AGENT

31–017   Add at the end of the paragraph: In *Skylight Maritime SA v Ascot Underwriting Ltd* [2005] P.N.L.R. 25, p.450, as in *Yonge v Toynbee* (in this paragraph in the main text), the defendant solicitor had warranted that he had authority to conduct litigation on behalf of his principal, costs which could not be recovered by way of a costs order against the supposed principal: see at *ibid.*, para.16. Here, however, the claim was likely to fail on account of the supposed principal's insolvency; for the relevance of the principal's insolvency see para.31–004 of the main text.

BOOK TWO
PART TWO
TORT

TORTS AFFECTING GOODS: DAMAGE AND DESTRUCTION

I. DAMAGE

1. NORMAL MEASURE

Insert a new note at the end of the paragraph: **32–009**

NOTE 53a: Lord Hope's stating at the start of his speech in *Lagden v O'Connor* [2004] 1 A.C. 1067, para.14, that *Lagden* was an appeal against the Court of Appeal's decision in *Burdis v Livsey* [2003] Q.B. 36, CA may confuse. The two cases were part of a number of test cases which had been heard together at Court of Appeal level and the issue in the *Lagden* appeal to the House of Lords was entirely different from what had been the issue in the *Burdis* appeal to the Court of Appeal. Indeed leave to appeal to the House of Lords was granted in *Lagden* and refused in *Burdis*: [2003] 1 W.L.R. 394. For *Lagden* see para.32–017A, below.

NOTE 55: Add at the end: *Performance Cars* was however held to be directly **32–010** in point in *Steel v Joy* [2004] 1 W.L.R. 3002, CA and was approved and followed: see para.6–021A, above.

2. CONSEQUENTIAL LOSSES

(1) *Expenses other than the cost of repair*

Insert a new paragraph after para.32–017:

32–017A However in *Lagden v O'Connor* [2004] 1 A.C. 1067 the House of Lords, by a majority, held the claimant entitled to recover the higher charges of the hire car company because he could not afford to hire a car at all. "Common fairness", said Lord Nicholls at para.6,

> "requires that if an innocent plaintiff cannot afford to pay car hire charges, so that left to himself he would be unable to obtain a replacement car to meet the need created by the negligent driver, then the damages payable under this head of loss should include the reasonable costs of a credit hire company".

Nor was the claimant required to account for the additional benefits that hiring from a credit hire company brought. The evidence showed, said Lord Hope, that he "had no choice but to use the services of the credit hire company and that, if he was to make use of these services, he had no way of avoiding the additional benefits that were provided to him": *ibid.*, para.35. The impecuniosity of the claimant made the case different from *Dimond v Lovell* [2002] 1 A.C. 384 which the House of Lords distinguished; for the abandonment by *Lagden* of the celebrated impecuniosity rule of *The Liesbosch* [1933] A.C. 449 see para.6–101A, above.

II. DESTRUCTION

1. NORMAL MEASURE

32–050 NOTE 60: Add at the end: That the bailor, apart from recovering for the loss to the bailee to whom it has to account, is entitled to recover for its own loss, if it can show any, is illustrated by *Re-Source America International Ltd v Platt Site Services Ltd* [2005] 2 Lloyd's Rep. 50, CA.

2. CONSEQUENTIAL LOSSES

(2) *Loss of profits of profit-earning chattels*

32–054 NOTE 86: Add at the end: But see now para.6–101A, above for the abandonment of the remoteness rule of *The Liesbosch* [1933] A.C. 449 in *Lagden v O'Connor* [2004] 1 A.C. 1067.

CHAPTER 33

TORTS AFFECTING GOODS: MISAPPROPRIATION

II. CONVERSION

1. NORMAL MEASURE

(1) *In general*

Insert a new note after the second sentence of the paragraph: **33–007**

NOTE 31a The question in *Lambeth LBC v Cumberbatch* [2005] EWCA Civ, July 11, CA was how to arrive at a valuation of converted unroadworthy vehicles due to be made roadworthy by the claimant vehicle repairer.

6. CONSEQUENTIAL LOSSES

NOTE 49: Add: In *Sandeman Coprimar SA v Transitos y Transportes Inte-* **33–066**
grales SL [2003] Q.B. 1270, CA the Court of Appeal undoubtedly accepted that in a negligent conversion the test was reasonable foreseeability: see *ibid.*, paras 25 to 31. The case is considered at paras 6–184A and 6–184B, above.

CHAPTER 34

TORTS AFFECTING LAND

I. DAMAGE

1. NORMAL MEASURE

(1) *In general*

34–004   Add at the end of the paragraph: The trial judge's award of diminution in value was set aside by the Court of Appeal in *Bryant v Macklin* [2005] EWCA Civ 762, June 23, and a substantially higher figure based on partial reinstatement substituted; see the case at para.34–011, below.

34–011   Add at the end of the paragraph: *Bryant v Macklin* [2005] EWCA Civ 762, June 23, is similar to *Scutt v Lomax* in that, the claimants' trees having been damaged by the defendants' animals breaking through the boundary between their two properties, only a partial replacement of trees was allowed by the Court of Appeal, based upon what was regarded as reasonable.

NOTE 61: Add at the end: And the same boost of the damages was made in the similar *Bryant v Macklin* [2005] EWCA Civ 762, June 23: see also at paras 34–018 and 34–037, below.

Insert a new paragraph after para.34–012:

Cases may arise in which there is, in addition, a degree of recovery for non-pecuniary loss, loss which tends to be classified in this context of damage to land as a loss of amenity, constituted by annoyance, inconvenience, discomfort and the like. The principal examples come from the law of nuisance, separately dealt with (see para.34–018 of the main text and para.34–018A, below), but the analogous tort of trespass to land has produced further illustrations (dealt with together with the nuisance cases).   **34–012A**

(3) *The particular case of nuisance*

NOTE 79: Add at the end: In *Abbahall Ltd v Smee* [2003] 2 E.G.L.R. 66, CA   **34–015**
the damages consisted of expenditure in abating a nuisance by repairing the roof of a building of which the claimant owned the ground floor and the defendant the upper floors, the main issue for the court being to decide upon the proper division of the expenditure between the parties.

NOTE 90: Add at the end: And in any event *The Liesbosch* has now been   **34–016**
departed from in *Lagden v O'Connor* [2004] 1 A.C. 1067: see para.6–101A, above.

NOTE 95: Insert at the beginning: And has now been buried by *Lagden v*   **34–017**
O'Connor [2004] 1 A.C. 1067: see para.6–101A, above.

Insert before the last sentence of the paragraph: *Bryant v Macklin* [2005]   **34–018**
EWCA Civ 762, June 23, is a factually similar case of trespass (at para.34–011, above) where the trial judge's award for loss of amenity of £3,000, following the award in the earlier case, was increased by the Court of Appeal to £12,000 as it was the claimants' home that was affected and not, as in the earlier case, a distant property which was only visited from time to time.

Insert a new paragraph after para.34–018:

Damages were awarded for a nuisance under three separate heads in *Dennis*   **34–018A**
v Ministry of Defence [2003] 2 E.G.L.R. 121 which were stated, in relation to the land, as loss of amenity, loss of use and loss of capital value. However, the trial judge rather curiously awarded what he called an "overview" figure, which amounted to £950,000, stating that he took into account the three identified heads of damage in arriving at his overall figure but that this was not just simply an addition of the three: *ibid.*, para.88. It was the level of aircraft noise created by the airfield operated by the defendant, constituting a very serious interference with the claimant's enjoyment of his property, which was held to amount to a legal nuisance entitling him to substantial damages. The loss of use is easily dealt with; it was based on the claimant's serious consideration of using the property for corporate entertaining to maximise

income and help make ends meet. The loss of capital value has the feature that it was held to be of limited duration, on the basis that the airfield would not continue after 2012 to operate in a noisy way. Accordingly, only a very small percentage of the significant reduction in the capital value of the land was awarded as the value would eventually be restored and it was unlikely that the claimant would wish to sell in the meantime: see *ibid.*, paras 83, 86 and 89. The loss of amenity is the most interesting. The judge said that if noise had formed the only head of damage he would have awarded £50,000 because it needed "not less than £50,000 to do justice to this loss of amenity if this aspect stood alone": para.89. This suggests that less than this amount is to be attributed to the loss of amenity within his grand total of £950,000 and one is also led to question why the amount awarded under this head should be in any way influenced by what is being awarded as compensation for the pecuniary losses. In any event, as the authorities in para.34–018 of the main text show, no other nuisance case has come up with anywhere near as high a non-pecuniary award, and the £50,000 is in stark contrast to the £10,000 in *Farley v Skinner* [2002] 2 A.C. 732 — aircraft noise in the context of a professional negligence claim — which their Lordships considered to be at the very top end of the scale and allowed to stand only because the case was special and exceptional: see para.29–045 of the main text. It may be, however, that their Lordships were thinking of contract where damages for non-pecuniary loss are more muted and could be said to be special and exceptional. It is also fair to say that the judge in *Dennis* did note the award in *Farley* but did not consider it in point or an apt comparison because he regarded the noise nuisance in *Dennis* as "testing the limits of tolerance": *ibid.*, para.85.

(4) *The particular case of infringement of human rights*

34–020   NOTE 16: Add at the end: Holding the defendant liable in nuisance in *Dennis v Ministry of Defence* [2003] 2 E.G.L.R. 121 (facts at para.34–018A, above) again obviated the need to consider the human rights position but the court stated that, should it be wrong on nuisance, the claimant would still succeed under the Human Rights Act: see *ibid.*, para.92.

Add at the end of the paragraph: The House of Lords has reversed the decision of the Court of Appeal, holding that the claimant could sustain neither a claim in nuisance nor one under the Human Rights Act: *Marcic v Thames Water Utilities Ltd* [2004] 2 A.C. 42. No issue of damages was discussed.

3. PROSPECTIVE LOSS

NOTE 85: Add at the end: Nor was the House of Lords required to address **34–031**
the issue by virtue of holding that claims neither in nuisance nor under the
Human Rights Act lay: *Marcic v Thames Water Utilities Ltd* [2004] 2 A.C. 42.

4. CLAIMANT WITH A LIMITED INTEREST

(2) *Persons not in occupation*

(a) Persons with a reversionary interest

Insert a new note after the second sentence of the paragraph: **34–034**

NOTE 88a: That the claimant was a reversioner in *Abbahall Ltd v Smee*
[2003] 2 E.G.L.R. 66, CA (facts at para.34–015, n.79, above) did not stand in
his way in his claim for expenditure in abating the nuisance: see *ibid.*, paras 6
and 7.

5. AGGRAVATION AND MITIGATION; EXEMPLARY DAMAGES

Add at the end of the paragraph: *Bryant v Macklin* [2005] EWCA Civ 762, **34–037**
June 23, is a factually similar case (at para.34–011, above) where the trial
judge's award for aggravated damages of £1,000, following the award in the
earlier case, was increased by the Court of Appeal to £4,000 since the aggravation by the defendants' deliberate and high-handed conduct was far greater
than in the earlier case.

II. OCCUPATION AND USER

3. PROSPECTIVE LOSS

Insert new paragraphs after para.35–052:

Recovery based on the principles of user and of the allied bargaining **34–052A**
opportunity (see paras 12–008 and 12–009 of the main text), with the damages still being regarded as compensatory rather than truly restitutionary,
appears in *Severn Trent Water Ltd v Barnes* [2004] EWCA Civ 570, May 13.
In laying a water main in the exercise of its statutory functions the defendant
water undertaker committed a trivial, accidental and unintentional trespass
by placing part of the main under the extreme corner of an over two-acre
parcel of the claimant's grazing land. As a statutory undertaker the defendant had been entitled to enter on land and do the mains work subject only

to service of notice on the landowner affected and, later, to payment to him of compensation which, in the absence of agreement, would be assessed by the Lands Tribunal. The defendant had not served notice on the claimant because unaware of his land ownership and, when the true position was discovered after the main had been constructed, he claimed damages. Three elements of damage appear in the claim. The first was the amount at which the Lands Tribunal would have assessed the statutory compensation payable had the defendant known of the claimant's ownership and served notice before the trespass. This was assessed at £110 and recovery of this amount was not in dispute. The second element was loss to the claimant of the opportunity to bargain over the proper compensation had he been given notice before the work was carried out, in effect the nuisance value of his claim to compensation over and above the £110. This was assessed by the judge at £500 and upheld by the Court of Appeal as appropriate damages for loss of bargaining opportunity. The third element was the alleged benefit obtained by the defendant from its use of the water main, claimed as restitutionary damages. This was assessed by the judge at £1,560 by a somewhat curious calculation which need not detain us since the Court of Appeal, after a full review of all the cases (see *ibid.*, paras 22 to 32), disallowed this part of the award. Having found for the claimant on the lost opportunity basis entitling him to recover a fair price, it was inappropriate for the judge to have topped up his award — the words of the Court of Appeal at *ibid.*, para.37 — by an amount based on benefit to the defendant. Whether the claimant could have claimed such benefit in lieu of lost opportunity damages was not fully debated.

34–052B   Whether one regards the damages awarded as compensatory or as restitutionary, this decision would seem to be correct. The essential difference between *Severn Trent* and all of the earlier cases (in the main text) where a defendant has trespassed on a claimant's land in order to carry out works bringing in profit is that Severn Trent under its statutory powers could require a landowner to give up to it the use of his land; the landowner had no choice in the matter. In these circumstances it is right to say that the landowner has lost the opportunity to negotiate compensation before the trespass; whereas in the other cases the opportunity is one that the claimant would not have wished to have taken, preferring to retain the enjoyment of his property without the defendant's proposed intrusion on it, here the claimant, with no choice but to let the defendant proceed, would have bargained for as much compensation as he could muster. At the same time the benefit to the statutory undertaker from its proceeding without notice is not such profit that it may have made from the tiny portion of its water main under the claimant's land — a profit which may have been small, even if assessable, despite the claimant's grandiose submissions — but is no more than the amount in compensation that it has saved itself by proceeding without giving notice. As Potter L.J. succinctly put it: "The financial advantage to Severn Trent in proceeding without payment was no more than the mirror image of the financial disadvantage to Mr. Barnes of being kept out of his money": *ibid.*, para.36.

The fact that in *Severn Trent* the defendant could require the claimant to give up the use of his land also serves to explain why the amount finally awarded was small compared with awards in other cases. This was, as the Court of Appeal pointed out at *ibid.*, para.39, not only because loss and benefit were insignificant but also because in all the authorities cited the defendant would have been unable to proceed without the claimant owner's permission thereby placing him in a much stronger position to negotiate a price or licence fee prior to trespass, being constrained only by market forces. **34–052C**

Insert after the first sentence of the paragraph: While there was no real or significant benefit to the defendant in *Severn Trent Water Ltd v Barnes* [2004] EWCA Civ 570, May 13, the Court of Appeal in its award continued to concentrate on user and compensation rather than benefit and restitution: see the case at para.34–052A, above. **34–053**

Chapter 35

TORTS CAUSING PERSONAL INJURY

I. FORMS OF AWARD AND OF COMPENSATION

2. PROVISIONAL AWARDS

NOTE 16: Add at the end: Provisional damages are not available where the chance is not deterioration in condition but the need for care and accommodation that will no longer be free: *Adan v Securicor Custodial Services Ltd* [2005] P.I.Q.R. P p.79. **35–006**

3. STRUCTURED SETTLEMENTS

NOTE 31: Add at the end: This recommendation has now become a requirement, by way of a Practice Direction supplementing CPR Pt 40. For more details see para.44–019Q, below. **35–010**

4. PERIODICAL PAYMENTS

Insert new paragraphs after para.35–018 (which take the place of paras 35–011 to 35–018 in the main text):

All the provisions on periodical payments are now in force but it has taken a good time for this to happen, a good time even after the Courts Bill (discussed in the main text at para.35–013 onwards) reached the statute book as the Courts Act 2003. A trio of statutory instruments, SI 2005/841, 910 and 911(together with a statutory instrument, SI 2005/547, which, because defective, was never brought into force) has been required. The first essential was to bring what are now sections, as opposed to clauses, 100 and 101, and with them the new ss.2, 2A and 2B of the Damages Act 1996, into force and this is achieved by a Commencement Order (SI 2005/910 (replacing part of SI 2005/547)) providing for ss.100 and 101 to come into force on April 1, 2005 (*ibid.*, para.3(w)). A further statutory instrument (SI 2005/911 (replacing part of SI 2005/547)), stated to come into force also on April 1, 2005 (*ibid.*, para.1), provides that **35–018A**

"the powers conferred by section 2(1) and (2) of the Damages Act 1996 [*viz.*, the powers relating to the awarding of periodical payments] shall be exercisable in proceedings whenever begun" (*ibid.*, para.11).

And a separate statutory instrument (SI 2005/841), required by s.2B of the Damages Act 1996 to deal with variation of periodical payments and curiously stated to come into force a specified number of days after the instrument was made, which, *mirabile dictu*, turns out to be April 1, 2005 (*ibid.*, para.1(1)), provides, by contrast, that

> "this Order [*viz.*, The Damages (Variation of Periodical Payments) Order 2005] applies to proceedings begun on or after the date on which it comes into force" (*ibid.* para.1(5)),

thereby ensuring that awards of periodical payments cannot be subject to later variation if the claim form in the case has been issued before April 1, 2005.

35–018B   In relation to the ordering of periodical payments, the central feature of the power given to the courts is that it is limited to "awarding damages for future pecuniary loss": Damages Act 1996, s.2(1). It is not intended to deal with either past pecuniary loss or with non-pecuniary loss by way of general damages, although it is provided that "other damages in respect of personal injury", *viz.*, damages other than damages for future pecuniary loss, may be awarded by way of periodical payments if the parties consent: *ibid.*, s.2(2). Thus damages for the loss of congenial employment — essentially non-pecuniary loss — cannot take the form of periodical payments. Nor, it would seem, can *Smith v Manchester* awards representing handicap in the labour market — it is so stated in the Judicial Studies Board's guidance document prepared by Judge Oliver-Jones Q.C. and Master Ungley (at para.13) — though it can surely be argued that such an award is for a future pecuniary loss though only a potential one.

35–018C   As to what matters are to be taken into account in considering whether to order periodical payments, guidance, formerly unavailable (see para.35–014 of the main text), is now provided by a new Section II to Pt 41 of the Civil Procedure Rules supplemented by a new Practice Direction, PD41B, although, as was already pointed out in the main text (again at para.35–014), these vital considerations should have been laid down in the primary legislation rather than be regulated by rules of procedure and Practice Directions. Turning first to the CPR provisions one finds that r.41.7, which is headed "Factors to be taken into account", simply says that, when considering in a particular case whether periodical payments or a lump sum is likely to be more appropriate and whether to order periodical payments,

> "the court shall have regard to all the circumstances of the case and in particular the form of award which best meets the claimant's needs, having regard to the factors set out in the practice direction".

One is thus moved down to the Practice Direction where one finds in PD41B, para.1, again under the heading "Factors to be taken into account", that there are in effect only two:

(1) the scale of the annual payments taking into account any deduction for contributory negligence: para.1(1); and

(2) the form of award preferred by the claimant and by the defendant and the reasons for their preferences, together with, in the case of the claimant, the nature of the financial advice received by him on the matter: para.1(2) and (3).

Some concern may be expressed about these two factors to be taken into account. As to the first factor, although the scale of the payments is to be considered by the court, it is unfortunate that there is not introduced, as has been proposed by some, a presumption in favour of periodical payments for large cases, say cases in excess of £250,000, with a countervailing presumption against them where the award for future pecuniary loss falls below the specified figure. Also it is not made clear how the existence of contributory negligence is to affect decisions as between lump sum and periodical payments. Contributory negligence is particularly important where the damages are being awarded to cover the cost of long-term care. Does the fact that periodical payments significantly reduced for contributory negligence will not cover the ongoing cost mean that the court should be moved towards awarding a traditional lump sum? Or can the court raid, as it were, the lump sum award for non-pecuniary loss, or possibly the lump sum for past gratuitous care which will not have been spent, in order to increase the level of periodical payments given for the future long-term care? Or would either of these possibilities require the consent of the parties? As to the second factor, since it appears that, for reasons set out elsewhere (at para.35–012 of the main text), the preference of the great majority of both claimants and defendants will be for a lump sum, paying too much attention to this by the courts could prove the death knell to the whole new system.

35–018D

In relation to the variation of periodical payments, guidance, again formerly unavailable (see para.35–015 of the main text), is now provided, by statutory instrument rather than by rules of procedure (contrast para.35–018C, above), as to what situations are to be taken as giving rise to the possibility of varying an award of periodical payments; again it may be emphasised that these vital considerations should have been laid down in the primary, rather than in secondary, legislation. Thus it is laid down in para.2 of the Damages (Variation of Periodical Payments) Order 2005 (referred to at para.35–018A, above) under the heading "Power to make variable orders" that the court, on a party's application, with the agreement of all parties or on its own initiative, may provide in an order for periodical payments for its variation

35–018E

"if there is proved or admitted to be a chance that at some definite or indefinite time in the future the claimant will —

(a) as a result of the act or omission which gave rise to the cause of action, develop some serious disease or suffer some serious deterioration, or

(b) enjoy some significant improvement in his physical or mental condition, where that condition had been adversely affected as a result of that act or omission".

35–018F   A whole series of serious criticisms of this provision, and those which follow it in the statutory instrument, may be advanced.

(1) The major criticism is of course that the scope for variation is much more limited than had been anticipated (see the discussion at para.35–015 of the main text), being restricted to changes in the claimant's condition, physical or mental. Why should this be the only change of circumstances envisaged by the legislation? Indeed it may be said that changes in the medical condition of the victims of a seriously disabling injury are rare. What is far more important is change in the care needs of the injured person. There may, for instance, be change of needs for equipment for the disabled, but perhaps the most important potential change is that caused by the unexpected death or departure of a spouse who has shouldered the caring and whose departure makes necessary for the injured person hospital or other institutional care which could be either very costly or, alternatively, free.

(2) It is further required that the chance of the change in the claimant's condition be envisaged and anticipated. Surely these provisions should deal with the unexpected as well as the anticipated and the variations should be intended to provide for what cannot be predicted.

(3) It is then provided, in para.5(b), that the court's order "must specify the disease or type of deterioration or improvement" envisaged. Yet it may not be possible to be sure of the disease or deterioration which may come about. And the provision in para.7 that

"a party may make only one application to vary a variable order in respect of each specified disease or type of deterioration or improvement"

is unnecessarily restrictive. Indeed there is too much of an attempt here simply to mirror the earlier provisions on entitlement to provisional damages (see paras 35–006 and 35–007 of the main text) which are in the nature of things bound to have a smaller compass and, moreover, have found little use in the 20 years that they have been in force.

35–018G   The other, clearly wise provisions referred to at para.35–016 of the main text have passed without alteration into the final legislation. This is true of the exemption of periodical payments from income tax (s.100 of the Courts Act 2003 appropriately amending s.329AA of the Income and Corporation Taxes Act 1988) and of the prevention of the assignment of the right to receive periodical payments without court approval (so provided in the Damages Act 1996, s.2(6)). As for the all-important provision that courts may not award periodical payments unless satisfied that continuity of payment is reasonably secure, this requirement is now firmly ensconced in the Damages Act 1996, s.2(3) while s.2(4), specifying the circumstances in which continuity of payment will be regarded as secure, covers self-funded periodical payments made by public sector bodies and guaranteed by a Minister of the Crown, periodical payments made by authorised insurers which are self-funded or paid by a life insurer under an annuity contract purchased by or on behalf of a defendant, and periodical payments by government or health service bodies.

A serious weakness in the legislation, as it had been proposed, is dealt with at para.35–017 of the main text; it is there pointed out that the so-called "close-matching" regulations will require courts to cater for inflation by using RPI, the retail price index, but that indexing by earnings inflation and, more particularly, health care inflation is needed for full compensation since they are significantly steeper. Now the Damages Act 1996, s.2(8) specifically provides that   **35–018H**

> "an order for periodical payments shall be treated as providing for the amount of payments to vary by reference to the retail prices index . . . at such times, and in such a manner, as may be determined by or in accordance with Civil Procedure Rules"

with s.2(9) going on to say that the order for periodical payments may disapply, or modify the effect of, s.2(8). This is then supplemented by CPR, r.41.8(1)(g) providing that the court's order must specify

> "that the amount of the payments shall vary annually with reference to the retail prices index, unless the court orders otherwise under s.2(9) of the Damages Act 1996".

Yet there would seem to be no good reason for disapplying s.2(8) so as to make no provision at all for increasing payments, and it is difficult to see, in the light of what has been referred to above from para.35–017 of the main text, how the effect of it could be modified so as to allow payments to rise by reference to the more favourable indices.

The subordinate legislation has fortunately paid heed, probably as a result of representations made, to the apparent lacuna in ss.100 and 101 in omitting provision for the dependants of claimants dying from their injury (a lacuna dealt with at para.35–018 of the main text). However, the solution is a curious one. It does not allow dependants (as proposed in the main text) an action under the Fatal Accidents Act after the death has come about. Instead, it requires the court to make provision for the dependants (should death result from the injury) at the time of the claim by the injured party. This is achieved by a combination of CPR, r.41.8(2) and PD41B, para.2(1). Read together the two provide that: **35–018I** "an order may be made ... where a dependant would have a claim under s.1 of the Fatal Accidents Act 1976 if the claimant had died at the time of the accident ... that ... part of the award shall continue after the claimant's death, for the benefit of the claimant's dependants . .. specify[ing] the relevant amount and duration of the payments ...".

But it surely would be better, and wiser, to wait until after the death before coming to a view as to what will be needed by the dependants and indeed as to who the dependants will then be.

35–018J   It is very early days for there to be much in the way of decisions on how this revolutionary scheme is working. For an illustration of a periodical payments award under the new regime see *Walton v Calderdale Healthcare NHS Trust* [2005] EWHC 1053 (QB), May 18 (at para.44–019G, below) where the claimant strongly supported such an award, on advice that a lump sum might well run out before his death, and the defendant did not oppose.

35–018K   Only the substance of the new provisions has been addressed above. Much of the complex rules which have made their appearance, whether in the statute, the statutory instrument, the Civil Procedure Rules or the Practice Directions, is procedural in nature. These aspects are dealt with, necessarily intertwined with some of the substantive matters considered above, in Book III on Procedure at paras 43–027A to 43–027B and paras 44–019A to 44–019P, below, where also more of the legislation, both primary and secondary, will be found set out in full than has been cited in the above discussion.

II. CERTAINTY OF LOSS

1. CHANGES BEFORE THE DECISION OF THE COURT OF FIRST INSTANCE

(a) Loss increased

35–028   NOTE 68: Add at the end: See too the two consecutive injuries in *Steel v Joy* [2004] 1 W.L.R. 3002, CA, at para.6–021A, above, where *Baker v Willoughby* was rightly considered not to be in point.

IV. LOSS OF EARNING CAPACITY AND RELATED BENEFITS

35–047   NOTE 65: Add at the end: Interest on past earnings lost is not on the gross earnings but on the net amount after the tax and national insurance contributions which the employer would have been obliged to deduct: *Bentwood Bros (Manchester) Ltd v Shepherd* [2003] I.C.R. 1000, CA.

Insert a new note after the third sentence of the paragraph: **35–048**

NOTE 65a: But care must be taken that the multiplier used for the DIY assessment is not too high: see *Chase International Express Ltd v McCrae* [2004] P.I.Q.R. P p.314, CA.

(A) GENERAL METHOD OF ASSESSMENT

Insert a new note after the first sentence of the paragraph: **35–051**

NOTE 81a: But merely to make a 5 per cent deduction from the total figure for two and a half years' earnings and 10 years' pension is unacceptable: Bentwood Bros (Manchester) Ltd v Shepherd [2003] I.C.R. 1000, CA.

NOTE 84: Add: Claims brought on behalf of children on account of their   **35–052** education being alleged to be inadequate present very difficult problems for damages assessment as was said in *Liennard v Slough BC* [2002] E.L.R. 527 (see *ibid.*, paras 167 to 172) and again in *Keating v London Borough of Bromley* (see *ibid.*, paras 199 to 204), in both of which the claim in fact failed, and in such cases the *Blamire* approach may be particularly appropriate. It was indeed said in *Liennard* that *Blamire* would have applied.

NOTE 87: Add: But in making an assessment of loss of earnings over a lifetime by the employment of a global lump sum, it may be prudent to check the proposed sum against the method of multiplicand and multiplier, so that in *Sharpe v Addison* [2004] P.N.L.R. 23, p.426, CA, what would have been an annual figure of £4,000 for the multiplicand was seen to be much too small: see paras 37 to 39, *per* Rix L.J.

Add at the end of the paragraph: By contrast, in *Chase International Express Ltd v McRae* [2004] P.I.Q.R. P p.314, CA the Court of Appeal overturned the trial's judge's assessment by use of the multiplicand/multiplier method in favour of, as it was put, a round sum as was done in *Blamire*, there being little or no reliable evidence before the judge of the claimant's preaccident employment history or his post-accident earning capacity: see *ibid.*, paras 14 to 16.

Insert in the text after the third sentence of the paragraph: **35–054**

A fifth edition appeared in November 2004. The references have been changed to fit this new edition: see below *passim*.

NOTE 97: Add: Table 26 in the new fifth edition.

(B) CALCULATION OF THE MULTIPLICAND AND OF THE MULTIPLIER

1. DIMINUTION IN EARNINGS: THE BASIC FACTOR FOR THE MULTIPLICAND

35–057 NOTE 10: Add: The attempt to get round this clear rule in *Cooke v United Bristol Healthcare NHS Trust* [2004] 1 W.L.R. 251, CA failed: see paras 35–104A and 35–104B, below.

NOTE 11: Add at the end: As to the need to deduct a claimant's travelling expenses from the amount he had been earning see *Eagle v Chambers (No.2)* [2004] 1 W.L.R. 3081, CA at paras 66 to 68. For the position where the claimant takes new employment and then loses it see *Morris v Richards* [2004] P.I.Q.R. Q p.30, CA at para.6–063, n.87, above.

Insert a new paragraph after para.35–059:

35–059A *Hewison v Meridian Shipping Services PTE Ltd* [2003] I.C.R. 766, CA raised the issue of the effect of illegality upon a lost earnings claim in a more difficult context. The claimant was injured at work in an accident for which the defendants, his employers, admitted liability. He had been employed for many years as a merchant seaman but he had indicated, falsely, to his employers that he did not suffer from epilepsy, a condition which prohibited his working as a seafarer. Some time after the accident he was dismissed after suffering an epileptic seizure at work. By a majority the Court of Appeal held that he was not entitled to claim for loss of earnings on the basis of his continuing to work until retirement age as a seaman. Although he would not be disentitled to damages for loss of earnings that he would otherwise have received by reason only of a collateral or insignificant illegality or unlawful act, here his deception of his employers was neither collateral, being central to his obtaining the earnings in question, nor insignificant, because of the potential risks involved.

3. ADJUSTMENTS FOR VARIATION IN ANNUAL EARNINGS LOSS

(1) *In general*

35–076 NOTE 3: Add at the end: But the multiplicand cannot be increased to take into account wage inflation in excess of retail price inflation: see *Cooke v United Bristol Healthcare NHS Trust* [2004] 1 W.L.R. 251, CA at paras 35–104A and 35–104B, below.

4. PERIOD OF YEARS OF CLAIMANT'S DISABILITY: THE BASIC FACTOR FOR THE MULTIPLIER

Add at the end of the paragraph: In the new, fifth edition this has indeed happened.   **35–082**

5. ADJUSTMENTS WHERE LIFE EXPECTANCY IS CUT DOWN BY THE INJURY

NOTE 66: Add: Lord Phillips in *Gregg v Scott* [2005] 2 A.C. 176, in empha-   **35–085** sising that the justification for awarding damages for the lost years' earnings is the protection of the dependants left through death without the person upon whom they depended and without a cause of action available in respect of the death, considered that it would be much better "if the claimant has no right to recover for such loss of earnings and the dependants' right to claim under section 1(1) of the Fatal Accidents Act 1976 subsisted despite the claimant's recovery of damages for his injury": *ibid.*, para.182.

Add at the end of the paragraph: It having again been emphasised by Lord   **35–090** Phillips in *Gregg v Scott* [2005] 2 A.C. 176 that their Lordships' earlier deci- sion in *Pickett v British Rail Engineering* [1980] A.C. 136 to allow damages for earnings in the lost years was justified because "only in this way could provision be made for the loss to be suffered by the dependants" (para.180), the refusal to award such damages in the case of a child where there are clearly to be no dependants should continue. Wages in heaven should not be awarded when they are not needed on earth.

6. THE APPROPRIATE DISCOUNT RATE FOR THE MULTIPLIER

Insert new paragraphs after para.35–104:

The level of discount rate cannot however be challenged so as again to   **35–104A** allow a lower rate to be used, and therefore a higher multiplier to be arrived at, on the basis that, earnings inflation being greater than retail price infla- tion, use of a discount rate geared to ILGS and therefore to inflation meas- ured by the retail price index does not reflect the true loss. The method of arriving at the multiplier was all worked out by the Lord Chancellor in set- ting the discount rate when no doubt well aware that his discount rate would not protect against earnings inflation. In these circumstances an attempt to bypass the proscription of adjustment of the multiplier for higher earnings inflation was made in *Cooke v United Bristol Healthcare NHS Trust* [2004] 1 W.L.R. 251, CA by proposing adjustment of the multiplicand on this account. *Cooke* was one of three cases in which the appeals were heard, and reported, together — the other two were *Sheppard v Stibbe* and *Page v Lee* — and the argument in all three was primarily in relation to the large care costs involved, health care inflation being even higher than earnings inflation. The argument however ran also to earnings in *Sheppard* where there was in addition to the claim for care costs a substantial claim for loss of earnings and pension: see *Cooke* at paras 4 and 21. For convenience, with the same issue involved, both earnings and care costs are dealt with here.

35–104B In *Cooke* evidence of great detail was laid before the court by a chartered accountant on behalf of the claimants in the form of tables giving revised multiplicands with stepped increases over time to reflect the faster rise in earnings — and the even faster rise in care costs — in comparison with the retail price index. This evidence was held to be inadmissible. It was a premise of the Lord Chancellor's order that the effects of inflation in assessing future loss were to be catered for solely by means of the multiplier controlled by the discount rate. The discount rate was intended to be the only factor in the computation yielding the claimant's lump sum to allow for future inflation and the multiplicand could not be taken as allowing for the same thing without usurping the basis on which the multiplier had been fixed. "The substance of these appeals", said Laws L.J., "constitutes an assault on Lord Irvine's discount rate, and on the efficacy of the 1996 Act itself": *ibid.*, para.30. The multiplicand could be adjusted for any prospect of increased earnings but it had necessarily to be treated as based on levels of earnings current at the time of trial.

7. ADJUSTMENTS TO THE MULTIPLIER FOR CONTINGENCIES

35–107 NOTE 38: Add: (5th ed. 2004) Tables 3 to 14 only.

NOTE 39: Add: (5th ed. 2004) Tables 15 to 26 only.

35–108 Substitute for the indented passage the following passage:

"[the tables] make reasonable provision for the levels of mortality which members of the population of England and Wales alive today may expect to experience in the future".

NOTE 44: Add: (5th ed. 2004), Explanatory Notes, Section A, para.20.

35–109 NOTE 50: Add: (5th ed. 2004), Explanatory Notes, Section A, para.20 (with "plaintiff" changed to "claimant').

35–110 NOTE 57: Add: (5th ed. 2004), Explanatory Notes, Section B, para.31 *et seq.*

35–112 NOTE 64: Add at the end: (5th ed. 2004), Explanatory Notes, Section B, paras 30 to 39.

NOTE 65: Add at the end: In the 5th edition of 2004 paras 36 and 38 become paras 32 and 33 and para.37 becomes para.32.

Add at the end of the paragraph: In *Herring v Ministry of Defence* [2004]   **35–113**
1 All E.R. 44, CA Potter L.J., with whose judgment the other Lord Justices
expressed agreement, pointed out, at *ibid.*, para.38, that the Ogden Tables
make it plain that on an average basis the discount appropriate for the possibility of a claimant's earning career being interrupted by illness and unemployment is small compared with levels traditionally applied. "In my view",
he added, "that is a matter that should be borne in mind by judges when considering the level of discount to be made for contingencies generally." The
trial judge's discount of 25 per cent was reduced to 10 per cent (*ibid.*,
para.38), the figure of 25 per cent being said to be "a gross departure from
that appropriate simply in respect of future illness and unemployment" (*ibid.*,
para.31).

NOTE 82: Add: In *Herring v Ministry of Defence* [2004] 1 All E.R. 44, CA   **35–115**
Potter L.J. said at para.29:

"It is perhaps no surprise that the figures based on research reveal low
appropriate discounts when averaged across the board. The observations
of Windeyer J. in *Bresatz v Przibilla* (1962) 108 C.L.R. 541 have for long
been quoted but perhaps insufficiently recognised so far as deductions
for contingencies are concerned."

9. NO SPECIFIC ADJUSTMENTS FOR INFLATION

Insert a new note after the penultimate sentence of the paragraph: **35–118**

NOTE 1a: But it cannot be said to be entirely solved; it is solved for retail
price inflation, not for the higher earnings inflation. *cf.* in particular *Cooke v
United Bristol Healthcare NHS Trust* [2004] 1 W.L.R. 251, CA at paras
35–104A and 35–104B, above.

(C) THE DEDUCTIBILITY OF COLLATERAL BENEFITS

1. INSURANCE MONEYS

NOTE 36: Add: But *McCamley* is no longer to be followed. The Court of   **35–124**
Appeal so decided in *Gaca v Pirelli General plc* [2004] 1 W.L.R. 2683, CA,
holding that the insurance exception to the deductibility rule did not apply
any more than the benevolence exception. See the case further at
para.35–134, below.

4. GRATUITOUS PAYMENTS PRIVATELY CONFERRED

35–134   Add at the end of the paragraph: The Court of Appeal has now in *Gaca v Pirelli General plc* [2004] 1 W.L.R. 2683, CA sensibly held that *McCamley v Cammell Laird Shipbuilders* had been wrongly decided and should no longer be followed. After an extensive review of the authorities Dyson L.J., who gave the leading judgment, concluded on similar facts to *McCamley* that

> "this case does not come within the benevolence exception because: (a) the payments were made by the tortfeasor; and (b) the payment of benefits under the insurance policy was not equivalent, or analogous, to payments made by third parties out of sympathy": *ibid.*, para.39.

5. MONETARY SOCIAL SECURITY BENEFITS

(2) *The present position*

(a) Benefits for which express legislative provision is made

(i) The rule as to deduction of benefits

35–139   Insert a new note in the last line of the paragraph after "on one side":

NOTE 17a: For some of the anomalies which appear in the operation of the 1997 Act where there has been a CPR Pt 36 payment see *Williams v Devon CC* [2003] P.I.Q.R. Q p.68, CA. For *Williams* see para.44–024, n.26 of the main text.

Add a new note at the end of the paragraph:

NOTE 17b: One aspect of the accounting does concern the claimant's damages and that is that, if the defendant challenges the Compensation Recovery Unit certificate and obtains an amended certificate of a reduced amount and a repayment, he must account to the claimant for the repayment. This may seem obvious but it took a lengthy consideration of the complex statutory provisions in *Bruce v Genesis Fast Food Ltd* [2004] P.I.Q.R. P p.113 to reach this conclusion. See too *R. (on the application of Soper) v Criminal Injuries Compensation Board* [2004] P.I.Q.R. Q p.1, CA, a judicial review of an award in which it was the amount of the benefits deducted which was challenged, and on more than one ground. If the claimant has received benefits but the defendant has been unable to make any deduction from the damages because for some reason the Compensation Recovery Unit certificate states that no benefits have been received, the court is prevented by s.17 of the 1997 Act (which see at para.35–147 of the main text) from itself making a deduction from the damages: *Eagle v Chambers (No.2)* [2004] 1 W.L.R. 3081, CA; see at *ibid.*, paras 13 and 53.

Add a new note at the end of the indented passage in the text: **35–140**

NOTE 17c: Earnings lost for the purposes of the 1997 Act were held by a majority in *Chatwin v Lowther* [2003] P.I.Q.R. Q p.84, CA to include the amount recovered for rent paid by the claimant to her business landlord which she would have been able to meet out of the business which her injuries had forced her to give up.

V. MEDICAL AND RELATED EXPENSES

(A) EXPENSES INCLUDED

1. MEDICAL EXPENSES

Substitute for the existing heading (2): (2) *Medical treatment and care provided privately and provided by the National Health Service or by local authorities*

Add at the end of the paragraph: A different result from *Woodrup* was **35–159** arrived at in *Howarth v Whittaker* [2003] Lloyd's Rep. Med. 235, where the court held the claimant entitled to 18 hours of weekly care assistance without any reduction in respect of the seven hours per week of free care assistance which the claimant was already receiving before the trial and which could continue in the future. The claimant's damages fell to be based on the cost of care for the full 18 hours since, apart from the fact that the free care assistance might be discontinued after the award of damages, the claimant should be allowed to have a single care regime controlled by his case manager involving as few carers as possible: see *ibid.*, para.29.

Insert new paragraphs after 35–159:

The position with the cost of care provided by local authorities differs **35–159A** from that with medical costs incurred by the National Health Service. Local authorities are under an obligation to provide care and accommodation for those in need of it but there is no provision equivalent to that of s.2(4) of the Law Reform (Personal Injuries) Act 1948 on the expenses of medical treatment and facilities, no provision, that is, enacting that the tortfeasor cannot allege that it would be unreasonable for the victim of the injury to incur the cost of private care. Where therefore the cost of private care has been incurred in the past or will be incurred in the future, it is always an issue whether the incurring of these private care costs is reasonable.

This issue dominated in *Sowden v Lodge* [2005] 1 W.L.R. 2129, CA. At first **35–159B** instance damages were based on local authority residential care rather than the much more expensive private residential care because it was held to be in the claimant's best interests to have the local authority residential arrangement but augmented — or, as is now said, "topped up" — by an amount designed to cover the extent by which the local authority care might fall short of the claimant's reasonable needs, thereby reducing the damages for care dramatically since, as the law still stands, the local authority care is free: see para. 35–207, below. On the appeal, however, the Court of Appeal held that, in determining whether a claimant was entitled to recover the proposed private cost, the test to be applied was whether the private residential care and accommodation chosen and claimed for was reasonable, there being a difference between what a claimant could establish as reasonable and what a judge concluded was in the claimant's best interests. Paternalism did not replace the right to make a reasonable choice. In general terms, the approach was to compare what a claimant could reasonably require with what a local authority, having regard to the uncertainties present, was likely to provide in the discharge of its duty. If the latter fell significantly short of the former, the tortfeasor must pay for the private arrangement unless augmentation, or "top up", from him would meet the claimant's reasonable requirements. However, the Court of Appeal was concerned about the practicability of the proposed augmentation and accordingly decided that the claimant should be allowed to try to demonstrate, before the trial judge, that the proposed augmentation was impracticable and that, if that were so, the balance was tipped towards a private arrangement. Moreover, the burden of proving that the local authority is able to provide some or all of the care is on the defendant; there was no such evidence in *Walton v Calderdale Healthcare NHS Trust* [2005] EWHC 1053 (QB), May 18.

35–159C Where the judge had held in *Eagle v Chambers (No.2)* [2004] 1 W.L.R. 3081, CA that the claimant needed a private care regime, it was for the defendant to show that particular services would have been available and would have been obtained on the National Health Service, or from social services. The defendant having failed to establish this, the claimant was entitled to recover the higher costs of obtaining these services privately.

2. RELATED EXPENSES

(1) *Expenses of financial management*

35–161 Insert a new note after the heading preceding this paragraph:

NOTE 72a: Other than the expenses of financial management awards for the expenses of care management are becoming increasingly common. *Tinsley v Sarkar* [2005] EWHC 192 (QB), February 18, where the assistance of an experienced brain injury case manager was required, is illustrative.

Add at the end of the paragraph: In *Willbye v Gibbons* [2004] P.I.Q.R. P p.227, CA, the amount which it was accepted that the claimant's solicitor receiver would cost had risen to over £88,000. Because the claimant had been held to be as much as 75 per cent contributorily negligent, only one-quarter of the amount would be available for this expenditure with the balance having to be paid out of the relatively modest award made under the other heads of damage. The defendant contended that in the claimant's own interests the costs of receivership should therefore be reduced. However, though the court expressed reservations about the claimant's future intentions on receivership, it appeared that she would wish to continue it. She was entitled to apply her damages how she wished and the defendant's contention was properly rejected: all at *ibid.*, para.18.

35–162 Insert before the last sentence of the paragraph: The courts have now sensibly taken the position suggested here in the text that with a discount rate geared to index-linked securities it is inappropriate to give claimants damages for the expense of investment advice. It was so held at first instance in *Page v Plymouth Hospitals NHS Trust* [2004] 3 All E.R. 367. Davis J. said, at *ibid.*, para.49, that

> "although the annual investment costs can be presented as an element of the multiplicand to which the appropriate multiplier is to be applied, in my judgment they are, for these purposes, in substance to be regarded as within the 'territory' . . . of the applicable discount rate"

so that the situation was therefore similar to that in *Cooke v United Bristol Healthcare NHS Trust* (which see at paras 35–104A and 35–104B, above). Later, in *Eagle v Chambers (No.2)* [2004] 1 W.L.R. 3081, CA, the Court of Appeal unanimously approved *Page* and held, by a majority, that the same rule should apply to a patient claimant in the hands of the Court of Protection. This was so even though a patient had no choice but to allow the Court of Protection to invest his damages more widely than in index-linked securities and so to incur fees for investment advice.

(B) GENERAL METHOD OF ASSESSMENT

35–172 Add at the end of the paragraph: However, there will be cases where the future uncertainties are too great to use the multiplicand/multiplier method of computation. This was held to be the position in *Willbye v Gibbons* [2004] P.I.Q.R. P p.227, CA where the claimant was a girl injured when aged 12 and at the time of trial some 10 years later receiving excellent support from her mother and the man with whom she was by then living. The judge below had been presented with a set of calculations of the extra assistance needed if she had children and if she was unsupported in later life by family, both of which were problematic, and the Court of Appeal held that it was wrong to make separate awards for such contingencies. Kennedy L.J. said, at para.16, that

> "all that can realistically be done is to increase to some extent the fund available to the [claimant] to satisfy her need for assistance in the future, recognising the possible ways in which demands may be made upon that fund, but not attempting to evaluate separate types of potential demand, because if potential demands are separately evaluated it may well turn out that there is duplication, or that substantial awards have been made in respect of contingencies which have never happened."

The Court of Appeal thus arrived at a global sum for future care which meant that the multiplicand/multiplier method did not feature in its pure form. *cf.* the same issue with loss of earnings at para.35–052 of the main text.

35–173   Add at the end of the paragraph: And as *Cooke v United Bristol Healthcare NHS Trust* [2004] 1 W.L.R. 251, CA establishes, no adjustment can be made to account for the discrepancy between retail price inflation, on which ILGS returns are based, and the much higher care costs inflation by tampering with the multiplicand. This is fully considered at paras 35–104A and 35–104B, above.

35–179   Insert a new note at the end of the last sentence but two of the paragraph:

NOTE 51a: But this is not the right approach if the need for extra care later is distinctly uncertain, making the multiplicand/multiplier method inappropriate: see *Willbye v Gibbons* [2004] P.I.Q.R. P p.227, CA at para.35–172, above.

(C) THE DEDUCTIBILITY OF COLLATERAL BENEFITS

4. CARE PROVIDED GRATUITOUSLY BY RELATIVES AND OTHERS

(1) *The provider of the care*

(a) Care by third parties

35–186   Add at the end of the paragraph: The argument that awards for gratuitous care should be reserved for very serious cases was roundly rejected in *Giambrone v JMC Holidays Ltd* [2004] 2 All E.R. 891, CA. See the decision at paras 35–193A to 35–193C, below.

(2) *Amount to be awarded*

35–192   Add at the end of the paragraph: The Court of Appeal in *Willbye v Gibbons* [2004] P.I.Q.R. P p.227, CA reiterated what had been said in *Evans* (in the main text) to the effect that there was no conventional discount and held the trial judge's deduction of 25 per cent in respect of past care to be a perfectly permissible approach: see *ibid.*, para.10. A discount of 25 per cent also appears in *Tinsley v Sarkar* [2005] EWHC 192 (QB), February 18: see *ibid.*, paras 31 to 33.

Insert new paragraphs after para.35–193:

35–193A   In *Giambrone v JMC Holidays Ltd* [2004] 2 All E.R. 891, CA, where the claimants, mainly young children, had developed gastroenteritis when on holiday abroad and were cared for by their parents on return home, the Court of

Appeal upheld the trial judge's award for the value of gratuitous care on the basis that such awards might be allowed if a claimant's illness or injury was sufficiently serious to give rise to a need for care and attendance significantly over and above that which would be given anyway in the ordinary course of family life. The court rejected the defendant's submission, based on certain equivocal passages in *Mills v British Rail Engineering Ltd* [1992] P.I.Q.R. Q p.130, CA, that awards to compensate for gratuitous care could only be made in very serious cases. Brooke L.J., with whose sole judgment the other members of the court agreed, asked where would be the borderline between cases justifying an award and cases for no award, and considered that to have "an arbitrary dividing line, which would be likely to differ from case to case, and from judge to judge, would be likely to bring the law into disrepute": *ibid.*, para.26.

At the same time the Court of Appeal considered that awards for gratuitous care in excess of £50 a week at present-day values in cases in which a child suffering from gastroenteritis receives care from the family should be reserved for cases more serious than the ones before the court. It was considered that such sum represented a fair and proportionate balance "between the consideration that some payment ought to be made for the unpleasant additional burden placed on the family carer and the consideration that the care is being rendered in a family context" and that "the remuneration on this account should be relatively modest": *ibid.*, para.33.   **35–193B**

The claims were in contract, against the holiday provider, but clearly the ruling applies equally to tort.   **35–193C**

5. MONETARY SOCIAL SECURITY BENEFITS

(2) *The current position*

(a) Benefits for which express legislative provision is made

(i) The rule as to deduction of benefits

Add a new note at the end of the paragraph: **35–195**

NOTE 44a: Medical as well as income benefits were among the recoverable benefits returned by the Compensation Recovery Unit to the defendant for which he was held accountable to the claimant in *Bruce v Genesis Fast Food Ltd* [2004] P.I.Q.R. P p.113; and medical benefits were the benefits the deduction of which was challenged on a judicial review of an award of criminal injuries compensation in *R. (on the application of Soper) v Criminal Injuries Compensation Board* [2004] P.I.Q.R. Q p.1, CA. See both cases at para.35–139, n.17b, above; and see also para.35–139, n.17a, above.

(ii) Various features of the rule

35–198   Add at the end of the paragraph: Nor was the claimant in *Eagle v Chambers (No.2)* [2004] 1 W.L.R. 3081, CA, required to use her mobility allowance to invest in the motability scheme which would provide her with less costly transport and thereby cut down her loss. This followed from giving a wide construction to s.17 of the 1997 Act which the House of Lords had already done in a different context: see at para.35–147 of the main text.

6. SOCIAL SECURITY BENEFITS OTHER THAN MONETARY

(1) Facilities provided by the National Health Service and by local authorities

35–205   Add at the end of the paragraph: On the second of the issues in *Firth* the case was followed in *Howarth v Whittaker* [2003] Lloyd's Rep. Med. 235 so as to refuse an indemnity to the claimant against the possibility of having to pay for his care, except that the concern was over past and not future care. The local authority, it was contended, might change its mind about past care which had been free and now seek to charge for it. Apart from regarding this as a fanciful and speculative possibility, the court considered that the request ran "wholly contrary to the well-established principle that in cases of this kind there should be finality in the litigation": *ibid.*, para.32.

35–207   NOTE 89: Add at the end: In *Howarth v Whittaker* [2003] Lloyd's Rep. Med. 235 *Firth* and *Bell* were relied on to argue that the claimant would still be able to obtain care assistance after the damages were awarded: see *ibid.*, para.28. As to the correctness of *Firth* and *Bell* this was not challenged in the Court of Appeal in *Sowden v Lodge* [2005] 1 W.L.R. 2129, CA — see *ibid.*, paras 7 and 89 — but Longmore L.J., at *ibid.*, para.89, made it clear that he thought it would be more appropriate for the legislation to provide that local authorities could recover the costs of care from the tortfeasor; see too Pill L.J. at *ibid.*, para.3, and also para.35–209A, below. For the complications of *Sowden* see the case at para.35–159B, above.

Add a new note at the end of the paragraph:

NOTE 89a: In *Tinsley v Sarkar* [2005] EWHC 192 (QB), February 18, the question was not whether the claimant would be required to pay for the care, as under the relevant statutory regime, different from the one applicable in *Firth* (at para.35–205 of the main text), the needed services were free of charge with no power of recoupment and no means testing; the question was whether the authority's limited resources, and other factors, would allow it to provide the needed services. After extended consideration the trial judge concluded that there was sufficient uncertainty to justify no reduction in the damages for care: see *ibid.*, paras 106 to 129.

Insert a new paragraph after para.35–209:

Still a better solution could be to entitle injured persons to care and accom- **35–209A**
modation from the local authority without payment and to award damages
for the cost of that care and accommodation to the local authority itself. One
local authority, required to pay for an impecunious injured person's care and
accommodation under the law as it stands, has now tried to achieve this result
by the pioneering method of bringing an action at common law against the
party liable for the injury, arguing that that party owed it a duty of care not
negligently to inflict an injury resulting in damage to it in the form of care
costs. Not surprisingly, the claim in *London Borough of Islington v University
College London Hospital NHS Trust* [2005] EWCA Civ 596, June 16, failed,
the Court of Appeal holding on policy grounds that there was no such duty
of care. In the light of the current inability of the National Health Service to
sue for its costs and the unavailability of a direct action to the private carer
for compensation for his or her care, to allow an action to the local authority would, in the words of Ouseley J. (*ibid.*, para.53), be "a leap too far". As
with the giving of a similar entitlement to the National Health Service, legislation will be required.

VI. NON-PECUNIARY DAMAGE

2. HEADS OF NON-PECUNIARY DAMAGE

NOTE 10: Add at the end: For the emerging possibility of other heads of **35–211**
non-pecuniary losses see 35–221A and 35–221B, below. General damages do
not have to be enhanced to reflect the insult sustained or the gravity of the
harm caused, these factors being the domain of aggravated and exemplary
damages: *Re Organ Retention Group Litigation* [2005] Q.B. 506, para.68 (facts
at para.11–015, n.65, above).

(2) *Loss of amenities of life*

NOTE 21: Add at the end: Separate awards tend to be made on this account: **35–215**
see para.35–221A, below.

3. VARIOUS ASPECTS OF THE NON-PECUNIARY AWARD

Insert new paragraphs after para.35–221:

Certain inroads are being made on the rule of a single sum for the total **35–221A**
non-pecuniary loss. Thus it seems to be becoming a feature of personal injury
cases where the claimant is no longer able to continue in his former employment to make a separate award under the rubric "loss of congenial employment". In *Willbye v Gibbons* [2004] P.I.Q.R. P p.227, CA, where the Court of

Appeal reduced an award of £15,000 on account of loss of congenial employment to £5,000, counsel had told the court (*ibid.*, para.11) that the highest award that he had been able to uncover for this was £10,000 and that awards rarely exceeded £5,000. This suggests that such awards are now not uncommon; and indeed one can trace the idea back about a decade: see *Hale v London Underground* [1993] P.I.Q.R. Q p.30 cited at para.35–215, n.21 of the main text. The possibility of an award for loss of congenial employment also appeared recently in *Chase International Express Ltd v McRae* [2004] P.I.Q.R. P p.314 although no award was in fact made there. This was because the Court of Appeal did not regard the claimant, who worked as a motor cycle courier, as having provided enough evidence to indicate that he enjoyed riding his motor cycle and found his work as a motor cycle courier extremely satisfying. Kennedy L.J. said at *ibid.*, 22:

> "The award can only be made to compensate a claimant for the loss of congenial employment, as the head of damages indicates. Any award for the interference with the satisfaction which a claimant gets, for example, out of the use of a motor cycle in his ordinary social life has to be compensated for under the head of pain, suffering and loss of amenities."

Yet why should there be a difference in the way of regarding the damages awarded between the joy of work and the joy of play? The professional motor cyclist seems to be no different from the professional violinist whose deprivation of the enjoyment of playing has often been regarded as compensable by way of loss of amenities. Yet it is clear that the courts are continuing to regard loss of congenial employment as a different category of non-pecuniary loss from loss of amenities.

35–221B   On a grander scale there is the decision of the House of Lords in *Rees v Darlington Memorial Hospital NHS Trust* [2004] 1 A.C. 309 to award to all parents, who by reason of clinical negligence have brought an unwanted child into the world, a sum of £15,000 in lieu of the costs of bringing up the child, to which they had formerly been held entitled: see *Rees* at paras 35–244A to 35–244C, below. Their Lordships did not classify this award as one for non-pecuniary loss but it is difficult to see how else it can be justified.

(5) *Relevance of manner in which injury inflicted*

35–226   NOTE 90: Add at the end: No award of aggravated damages could arise for injury negligently inflicted: *Re Organ Retention Group Litigation* [2005] Q.B. 506, para.264 (facts at para.11–015, n.65, above).

(6) *Relevance of receipt of social security benefits*

35–227   NOTE 94: Add: See too para.35–139, n.17a, above.

4. LEVEL OF AWARDS

Insert after the second sentence of the paragraph: The seventh edition appeared in September 2004.   **35–229**

Insert before the last sentence of the paragraph: In the seventh edition of September 2004 the brackets for quadriplegia and severe brain damage are slightly higher, with quadriplegia at £175,000 to £220,000 and severe brain damage at £155,000 to £220,000. See *Guidelines* (2004), p.3 and p.5, respectively.   **35–236**

VII. ENVOI: THE PARTICULAR CASE OF CLAIMS BY PARENTS ARISING OUT OF THE BIRTH OF THEIR CHILDREN

(2) *Development and dénouement*

Insert a new note at the end of the paragraph: **35–244**

NOTE 43a: The High Court of Australia in *Cattanach v Melchior* [2003] Lloyd's Rep. Med. 447, HCA has, by a bare majority of a court of seven, declined to follow *McFarlane*.

Insert new paragraphs after para.35–244:

In *Rees v Darlington Memorial Hospital NHS Trust* [2004] 1 A.C. 309 the   **35–244A**
House of Lords followed and applied *McFarlane*, rejecting an invitation to depart from the decision pursuant to the familiar 1966 Practice Statement, a rejection which could very reasonably be expected with *McFarlane* decided only four years earlier. *Rees* concerned a claimant who was a disabled mother and the House, by a bare majority of four to three, held that the *McFarlane* ruling nevertheless applied. This aspect of the case is documented later (see para.35–251A, below). What requires to be noted here is that the majority held that, although there could be no award for the additional costs of upbringing attributable to the mother's disability, there should nevertheless be a conventional award to reflect some recognition of the wrong done and that this conventional award should apply in a *McFarlane*-type case as much as in a *Rees*-type case. For Lord Bingham, who was the first proponent in the House of the conventional award, said that it should be made "in all cases such as these" (*Rees* para.8) and that it should apply "without differentia-tion" (*ibid.*, para.9) to cases where child or parent was healthy and to cases where child or parent was disabled.

The precise purpose of the conventional award, the suggestion for which   **35–244B**
had earlier been put forward by Lord Millett in *McFarlane* itself but not there taken up, is variously stated by those of their Lordships who were in the majority. For Lord Bingham it was designed to deal with the loss represented

by the denial to the parent of the opportunity to live her life in the way that she wished and planned (*Rees* para.8); for Lord Nicholls it was in recognition of the parent having suffered a legal wrong having far-reaching effects on her and her family (*ibid.*, para.17); for Lord Millett it was for the denial of the right to limit the size of the family as an important aspect of personal autonomy (*ibid.*, para.123); for Lord Scott it was for the frustration of the expected benefit to be derived from being safeguarded from conception (*ibid.*, para.148). The amount proposed by Lord Bingham for the conventional award, and concurred in by the other members of the majority, was £15,000.

35–244C   The creation of such a conventional award marks a break from established principles of damages. It would fall within the accepted bounds of damages if it could be seen as an element of non-pecuniary loss, akin to loss of amenity, but Lord Bingham was careful to say that "the conventional award would not be, and would not be intended to be, compensatory" (*ibid.*, para.8) while Lord Millett spoke of "a purely conventional [figure] which should not be susceptible of increase or decrease by reference to the circumstances of the particular case" (*ibid.*, para.125). Both Lord Steyn and Lord Hope, in the minority on the main decision not to award the additional costs of upbringing, spoke in strong and convincing terms against the invention of the conventional award (see *ibid.*, paras 40 to 47 and paras 70 to 77 respectively), regarding the idea of such an award as contrary to principle. To Lord Hope, disturbed by his inability to find any consistent or coherent *ratio* in support of the conventional award in the speeches of the majority, the idea of a non-compensatory award departed from "the principle which has always guided the common law in its approach to the assessment of damages"; *ibid.*, para.74. However, it looks as if the conventional award is here to stay even though only endorsed, after little argument and no rigorous examination of the competing positions, by a bare majority in *Rees* and, in the estimation of Lord Nicholls there (*ibid.*, para.41), running counter to the views of all of their Lordships in *McFarlane* other than, predictably, Lord Millett.

(3) *Aftermath*

(b) Limited recovery where there is disablement

(i) *The disabled child*

Insert new paragraphs after para.35–250:

35–250A   The fate of *Parkinson v St James and Seacroft University Hospital NHS Trust* [2002] Q.B. 266, CA — and of *Rand, Hardman, Lee* and *Groom*: all at paras 35–248 and 35–249 of the main text — now lies in the balance. In *Rees v Darlington Memorial Hospital NHS Trust* [2004] 1 A.C. 309, in reversing the Court of Appeal, by a majority of four to three, so as to deny recovery for the extra costs of upbringing to the disabled parent (see para.35–251A, below), their Lordships *en passant* considered *Parkinson* and the case of the disabled child, putting forward a variety of views as to how such a case should be dealt with. The minority of three not surprisingly considered *Parkinson* to be right — Lord Steyn at *Rees* para.35, Lord Hope at *ibid.*, para.57 and Lord Hutton at *ibid.*, para.91 — since they were deciding in *Rees* in favour of the disabled parent. Similarly, there were three of the majority who considered *Parkinson* to be wrong, Lord Scott expressly at *Rees* para.145, and Lord Bingham and Lord Nicholls by clear implication as they both said they would apply the same rule whether it was the child or the mother who was disabled: see *ibid.*, para.9 and para.18 respectively. However, Lord Millett wished to keep open the question whether *Parkinson* was rightly decided — at *Rees* para.112 — so there is no clear majority in either direction to guide the lower courts or indeed a differently constituted House of Lords.

The fate of the first instance cases of failure to warn of disability rather than failure to sterilise — *Rand*, *Hardman* and *Lee* at para.35–248 of the main text — are rather less in the balance than the fate of the Court of Appeal's *Parkinson*. This is because Lord Scott in *Rees* drew a distinction turning on whether the medical treatment sought was simply in order to avoid conception or was because of a fear that a child would be born disabled: *ibid.*, para.145. If Lord Scott favoured the claimant, as he clearly did, in the case of failed sterilisation where the parties' minds had been directed to disability, he would surely regard the case of a failure to warn of disability in the same light. Accordingly, there can be found in *Rees* a majority of four to two in favour of *Rand*, *Hardman* and *Lee*, Lord Scott and the minority of three in *Rees* being ranged against Lord Bingham and Lord Nicholls determined to have a uniform rule, with Lord Millett still on the fence. **35–250B**

The result of all this is that we do not really know where we now are with the disabled child. The House of Lords has left a very muddled position for lower courts to resolve and interpret. Moreover, it is not yet clear whether, if a mother is held still to be entitled to the additional costs of upbringing where there is disablement, she will be awarded the conventional £15,000 (see para.35–244B, above) in addition. Presumably not. **35–250C**

(ii) The disabled parent

Insert a new paragraph after para.35–251:

The House of Lords has, by a majority of four to three, reversed the Court of Appeal in *Rees v Darlington Memorial Hospital NHS Trust* [2004] 1 A.C. 309. No longer entitled to the additional costs of bringing up the child, the parents will now be entitled to a conventional award of £15,000 as a measure of recognition of their injury and loss: see para.35–244A, above. **35–251A**

CHAPTER 36

TORTS CAUSING DEATH

I. CLAIMS FOR THE BENEFIT OF THE DECEASED'S DEPENDANTS

36–004   Add at the end of the paragraph: Fortunately, fatal accidents have been brought in. Indeed they have always been in, but this was not immediately, or at all, clear from the wording in ss.100 and 101 of what is now the Courts Act 2003 which in setting out the new sections for substitution in the Damages Act 1996 refer throughout only to personal injury. To see that the coverage goes beyond personal injury one has to go to the interpretation section in the original Damages Act 1996, s.7, which provides in subs.(1) that

> "references to a claim or action for personal injury include references . . . to a claim or action brought by virtue of the Fatal Accidents Act 1976."

Then it is seen that, for periodical payments, this is not a very felicitous way to bring in fatal accidents because, while the sole reference to personal injury in s.2 of the original Damages Act 1996 is to "a court awarding damages in an action for personal injury" — so that the rule propounded there clearly is to be applied to fatal accident claims — in the new s.2 the sole references, in subs.(1) and again in subs.(2), are to "a court awarding . . . damages . . . for personal injury" — so that it could be said that, there being no reference to a claim or action for personal injury, the section does not succeed in bringing fatal accidents within its compass. It is highly unlikely, however, that such a technical argument would prevail.

(A) THE STATUTORY ACTION

1. The Entitled Dependants

Insert a new note after the citation of s.1(3)(b)(ii):   **36–006**

Note 18a: Living in the same household was strictly interpreted in *Kotke v Saffirini* [2005] EWCA Civ 221, March 9, causing the claim to fail.

2. The Entitlement of the Dependants

(1) *Entitlement where no entitlement of deceased at death*

Note 49: Add at the end: Moreover, Lord Phillips has now said in *Gregg v*   **36–011**
Scott [2005] 2 A.C. 176, at para.182, that he is not persuaded that this solution "could not be achieved by a purposive construction of that section", *viz.*, s.1(1) of the Fatal Accidents Act 1976.

(2) *Entitlement where limited entitlement of deceased at death*

Note 54: Insert after the reference to *Newman v Folkes*: and *Hewitson v*   **36–014**
Meridian Shipping Services PTE Ltd [2003] I.C.R. 766, CA.

(B) THE STATUTORY MEASURE OF DAMAGES

Add at the end: A further type of loss for which damages were not recov-   **36–018**
erable made its appearance in *Batt v Highgate Private Hospital* [2005] P.I.Q.R. Q p.1 where an attempt was made to recover the expense of the negligently performed operation which itself had led to the death. As was rightly held, this could not be regarded as constituting part of the value of the dependency. See the case further on this at para.2–052, n.13, above and para.36–123, below.

1. Losses in Respect of which Damages are Not Recoverable or are Recoverable only within Limits

(1) *Non-pecuniary loss, except to a parent or child for bereavement*

Note 96: Add at the end: More satisfactory results would be arrived at if   **36–020**
the decisions on damages were left to the court; this is the position in Scotland. Thus in *Shaher v British Aerospace Flying College Ltd*, 2003 S.L.T. 791 £20,000 was awarded to each of the parents of a son killed at 19 in a flying accident; and there have been higher awards.

2. THE VALUE OF THE DEPENDENCY

(1) *The preliminary problem of certainty of loss*

(c) Changes after the litigation has ended

36–036   Add at the end of the paragraph: Fortunately, fatal accidents do appear to be included in the Courts Act 2003 as enacted; for details see para.36–004, above.

(2) *General method of assessment*

36–040   NOTE 89: Add at the end: Now in their fifth edition of 2004.

(3) *Calculation of the multiplicand and of the multiplier*

(b) Period of years of lost dependency: the basic factor for the multiplier

(ii) Assessment as from date of death

36–053   NOTE 50: Now fifth edition (2004).

36–055   NOTE 53: Add at the end: See para.22 of the Introduction in the new edition of 2004.

(4) *Particular relationships*

(b) Death of wife, death of mother

(i) Wife and mother

36–084   Insert before the last sentence of the paragraph: In *Batt v Highgate Private Hospital* [2005] P.I.Q.R. Q p.1 it was held that it was not reasonable for the father to have given up his job to look after his daughter so that the assessment was based on the cost of commercial care which was very much less than the amount the father had been earning: see at *ibid.* paras 24 to 32.

II. CLAIMS SURVIVING THE DEATH FOR THE BENEFIT OF THE DECEASED'S ESTATE

36–116   Add a new note at the end of the paragraph:

NOTE 77a: One would expect the new provisions in the Courts Act 2003 as to the awarding of periodical payments — achieved by the substitution of a new s.2 of the Damages Act 1996 for the old section — to apply automatically to actions by the estate since these are in effect actions for personal injuries which have survived the death. That the new provisions do apply is however spelt out in s.7(1) of the 1996 Act where it is provided that

> "references to a claim or action for personal injury include references to such a claim or action brought by virtue of the Law Reform (Miscellaneous Provisions) Act 1934 . . .".

Compare in this connection para.36–004, above in relation to Fatal Accidents Act claims. But all this is fairly academic since, after the barring of damages for loss of income after death in actions by the estate (see para.36–119 of the main text), there can be little, if any, scope for periodical payments in survival claims.

2. ACCRUED LOSSES OF THE DECEASED

(1) *Pecuniary losses*

Insert a new note at the end of the first sentence of the paragraph: **36–123**

NOTE 85a: But the attempt in *Batt v Highgate Private Hospital* [2005] P.I.Q.R Qp.1 to have awarded as damages in the survival claim the deceased's expenses of the negligently performed operation which led to her death rightly failed. See the case further on this at para.2–052, n.13, and para.36–018, above.

CHAPTER 37

ASSAULT AND FALSE IMPRISONMENT

I. ASSAULT

1. HEADS OF DAMAGE

37–001   Insert a new note at the end of the penultimate sentence of the paragraph:

NOTE 2a: But rather curiously the Court of Appeal has now indicated in *Richardson v Howie* [2005] P.I.Q.R. Q p.48, CA that aggravated damages should not generally be awarded in assault cases: see paras 37–003A to 37–003E, below.

2. AGGRAVATION AND MITIGATION

(a) Aggravation of damage

37–003   Add at the end of the paragraph: In the curious case of *Shah v Gale* [2005] EWHC 1087 (QB), May 27 (facts at para.44–023B, below), where the terrifying assault brought about the near immediate murder of the victim, the time factor did not allow the trial judge to award more than £2,750, £2,000 of which was expressed to be aggravated damages.

Insert new paragraphs after para.37–003:

37–003A   The Court of Appeal has heralded a change by holding that in cases of assault it is in general inappropriate to award aggravated damages on top of, and in addition to, damages for injured feelings. In *Richardson v Howie* [2005] P.I.Q.R. Q p.48, CA the assault took place in this fashion. While a couple described as being in a volatile relationship were holidaying far from home in the Caribbean, the man made a frenzied and spiteful attack on the woman with a glass bottle causing permanent scarring injuries. The trial judge awarded £10,000, which amount included £5,000 by way of aggravated damages. On appeal the defendant contended that any damages for the injury to the claimant's feelings should be encompassed within the award for general damages and that it was wrong in principle to make an award for aggravated damages. The Court of Appeal agreed.

Thomas L.J., delivering the judgment of the two-man court, recited the details of the various first instance assault cases in which aggravated damages have been awarded as cited at paras 37–002 and 37–003 of the main text — *W v Meah* [1986] 1 All E.R. 935, Appleton v Garrett [1996] P.I.Q.R. P p.1 and the earlier *Westwood v Hardy* [1964] C.L.Y. 994 — although the Court of Appeal decision cited in para.37–003 of *Hsu v Commissioner of Police of the Metropolis* [1998] Q.B. 498, CA, which also involved assault though together with wrongful arrest and false imprisonment, is ignored. After going through these authorities Thomas L.J. continued, at para.23: **37–003B**

> "It is and must be accepted that at least in cases of assault and similar torts, it is appropriate to compensate for injury to feelings including the indignity, mental suffering, humiliation or distress that might be caused by such an attack, as well as anger or indignation arising from the circumstances of the attack. It is also now clearly accepted that aggravated damages are in essence compensatory in cases of assault. Therefore we consider that a court should not characterise the award of damages for injury to feelings, including any indignity, mental suffering, distress, humiliation or anger and indignation that might be caused by such an attack, as aggravated damages; a court should bring that element of compensatory damages for injured feelings into account as part of the general damages awarded. It is, we consider, no longer appropriate to characterise the award of the damages for injury to feelings as aggravated damages, except possibly in a wholly exceptional case."

The Court of Appeal considered that an overall award of £10,000, as made by the judge, was far too high and substituted an award of £4,500 general damages.

It is difficult to follow the progress of the Court of Appeal's reasoning here. The classification of damages given for injured feelings as compensatory and the classification of aggravated damages as compensatory does not mean that the one is not independent of the other and that the one should be subsumed within the other. If the scale or the horror of the assault increases the injury to the claimant's feelings, the damage is aggravated, and hence the damages are aggravated, and the courts have recognised this in their awards. It is true that there does not have to be an amount awarded for aggravated damages **37–003C** separate from the basic award for injury to feelings (although the Court of Appeal have recommended this in the context of malicious prosecution) — indeed there was no separate award either in *Meah* or in *Hsu* (see para.37–003B, above) — but the concept of aggravated damages has not only been long recognised but was emphasised and highlighted by Lord Devlin when declaring exemplary damages anomalous in his speech in *Rookes v Barnard* [1964] A.C. 1129, the speech with which Thomas L.J. said it is necessary to begin: [2005] P.I.Q.R. Q p.48, CA, para.16. Aggravated damages should surely be retained in assault cases.

37–003D   Moreover, the removal of aggravated damages from the tort of assault will create a tension, indeed an inconsistency, between it and other torts where aggravated damages have had judicial blessing by first instance judges and by the Court of Appeal alike. Quite apart from defamation, malicious prosecution, false imprisonment and the statutory torts of discrimination in all of which the writ of aggravated damages undoubtedly runs, if the Court of Appeal is prepared to award aggravated damages against a defendant who damages land (see para.34–037 of the main text) and against a defendant who evicts from land (see paras 34–057 to 34–058 of the main text) how much more should such damages be available where the damage is to the person.

37–003E   It is also going to be difficult to know at what point we arrive at the exceptional category, which the Court of Appeal rather reluctantly recognises as still allowing aggravated damages. Thomas L.J.'s recital of the details of the various first instance cases in which aggravated damages have been awarded (see para.37–003B, above), all of which involved very serious assaults, does not make it clear whether the Court of Appeal is approving or disapproving of them. Are they within the exceptional category and accordingly endorsed, or are they not and therefore now to be considered as wrongly decided?

II. FALSE IMPRISONMENT

1. HEADS OF DAMAGE

37–008   NOTE 37: Add: The £1,500 awarded at first instance in *Taylor v Chief Constable of Thames Valley Police* [2004] 1 W.L.R. 3155, CA for some four hours of false imprisonment of a 10-year-old boy is consistent with this scale since it covered trespass to the person and assault as well. It had however to be reduced as on appeal there was held to be only one hour of unlawful detention: see *ibid.*, para.55.

II. SLANDERS ACTIONABLE *PER SE* AND LIBEL

1. LEVEL OF AWARDS

Insert a new note at the end of the second sentence:　　　　　　**39–024**

NOTE 27a: Their Lordships in *The Gleaner Co Ltd v Abrahams* [2004] 1 A.C. 628, PC said that they endorsed the ruling in the Jamaican Court of Appeal, consistent with *Rantzen*, that other jury libel awards should not be revealed to the jury, reference to appeal awards not arising as the Jamaican Court of Appeal did not have power to substitute its own award: see *ibid.*, para.58.

NOTE 30: Add at the end: By the time of *Kiam v MGN Ltd* [2003] Q.B. 281, CA, Lord Hoffmann noted in *The Gleaner Co Ltd v Abrahams* [2004] 1 A.C. 628, PC at para.47, the number had increased only to six.

NOTE 35: Add: By contrast, the Jamaican courts have retained their posi-　　**39–025** tion of not revealing personal injury awards to juries and their Lordships in *The Gleaner Co Ltd v Abrahams* [2004] 1 A.C. 628, PC have endorsed Jamaica's entitlement to consider that no change in practice was desirable (*ibid.*, para.63). The submission that the rejection of guidance from personal injury awards was an error of law was firmly rejected. No question of legal principle was involved; "whether a link", said Lord Hoffmann delivering the judgment of the Board, "should be established between defamation awards and personal injury awards is a question of policy": *ibid.*, para.62. Their Lordships said that they expressed no view on the current practice in England (*ibid.*, para.50). Nevertheless Lord Hoffmann's rigorous analysis of the differences between awards in these two very different fields (see *ibid.*, paras 49 to 56) may be thought to convey a certain leaning towards favouring the Jamaican, and former English, solution to what he regarded as a controversial question.

Insert new paragraphs after para.39–026:

39–026A   Eady J. has recognised in a number of his judgments that today the ceiling for compensatory damages in defamation is in the region of £200,000. He did so in *Cleese v Clark* [2004] E.M.L.R. 3, p.37 (at *ibid.*, para.33), in *Abu v MGN Ltd* [2003] 1 W.L.R. 2201 (at *ibid.*, para.6) and earlier in *Lillie and Reed v Newcastle City Council* [2002] EWHC 1600 (QB), July 30 (at *ibid.*, para.1550), Lord Hoffmann in *The Gleaner Co Ltd v Abrahams* [2004] 1 A.C. 628, PC citing this last reference without disapproval (at *ibid.*, para.49). Indeed in *Lillie and Reed*, an appalling case of subjection to accusations of child abuse by the City Council and an investigating review body, £200,000 was awarded by Eady J. to each of the two claimants against the four members of the review body whom he held to have acted with malice. By contrast, in *Campbell v News Group Newspapers Ltd* [2002] E.M.L.R. 43, p.966, CA, a jury award of £350,000 was reduced by the Court of Appeal to £30,000, but the case did involve misdirection and also misconduct by the claimant. The court stated at *ibid.*, para.26 that in an annex, Annex A, "we examine in greater detail the legal principles which govern libel damages". The downturn in the level of damages is specifically taken account of by Eady J. when he awarded £150,000 to the controversial George Galloway, who had been Labour Member of Parliament for Glasgow, on account of a libel that he was in the pay of Saddam Hussein: *Galloway v Telegraph Group* [2005] E.M.L.R. 7, p.115.

39–026B   This ceiling of £200,000 equates with that for awards for non-pecuniary loss in personal injury cases laid down by the Court of Appeal in *Heil v Rankin* [2001] Q.B. 272, CA: see para.35–234, above. *Gleaner* however shows that this move to smaller awards may not be reflected in Commonwealth countries, the award endorsed by the Jamaican Court of Appeal in *Gleaner* being of 35 million Jamaican dollars, the equivalent at the time of £533,000, while the award of the jury at the trial, which was set aside, had been as much as 80.7 million Jamaican dollars, the equivalent at the time of £1.2 million. The Judicial Committee of the Privy Council dismissed the defendant's appeal and upheld the Court of Appeal's award, saying in effect that the matter was one for Jamaica, a question of policy rather than of law. *Cf.* a related aspect of the case at para.39–025, n.35, above, and compare the earlier similar approach of their Lordships' Board to awards of exemplary awards in Australia, at para.11–005 of the main text.

2. HEADS OF DAMAGE

(1) *Injury to reputation*

Insert before the last sentence of the paragraph: One feature of these **39–027** damages, peculiar to defamation, which may make for high awards is that they must serve to show that the claimant's reputation is unsullied. As Lord Hoffmann put it in *The Gleaner Co Ltd v Abrahams* [2004] 1 A.C. 628, PC at para.55: "The damages must be sufficient to demonstrate to the public that the plaintiff's reputation has been vindicated. Particularly if the defendant has not apologised and withdrawn the defamatory allegations, the award must show that they have been publicly proclaimed to have inflicted a serious injury."

(2) *Injury to feelings*

Add at the end of the paragraph: *Cleese v Clark* [2004] E.M.L.R. 3, p.37, **39–029** an assessment of compensation under the new offer of amends procedure (for which see para.39–052 of the main text), is another case in which the injury to feelings easily outweighed the injury to reputation, the allegations against the claimant comedian, actor and writer in the defendant's newspaper article being said to be very much at the lower end of gravity: see *ibid.*, paras 39 and 42.

(4) *Pecuniary loss*

NOTE 63: Add at the end: When in *Collins Stewart Ltd v Financial Times* **39–031** *Ltd* [2005] E.M.L.R. 5, p.64 the claimant company attempted to show pecuniary loss by the fall in its share price as reflecting the loss of future revenues, the claim for special damages on this basis was struck out because as a suggested measure of damages it was too uncertain to be acceptable.

4. PLEADING AND PROOF OF DAMAGE

NOTE 69: Add at the end: The Court of Appeal has confirmed that the pre- **39–034** sumption of damage continues to exist, is irrebuttable, and is not abrogated by the arrival of the Human Rights Act: *Jameel v Dow Jones & Co Inc* [2005] 2 W.L.R. 1614, CA; *Jameel v Wall Street Journal Europe SPRL* [2005] 2 W.L.R. 1577, CA.

5. AGGRAVATION AND MITIGATION: RELEVANCE OF THE CONDUCT, CHARACTER
AND CIRCUMSTANCES OF THE PARTIES

39–036   Insert a new note at the end of the paragraph:

NOTE 78a: Matters in aggravation increased the damages in *Galloway v
Telegraph Group* [2005] E.M.L.R. 7, p.115; see the case at para.39–026A,
above. By contrast, aggravated damages were refused in *Rackham v Sandy*
[2005] EWHC 482 (QB), March 23; see *ibid.,* para.124.

(1) *The defendant's conduct: malice*

(b) Evidence to disprove malice in mitigation of damages

(iv) Apology or offer of amends by the defendant

39–052   Insert a new note at the end of the penultimate sentence of the paragraph:

NOTE 55a: Offering to make amends will generally, if not always, entail a
giving of compensation and s.3(5) of the Defamation Act 1996 provides that,
where the parties are not in agreement on the amount to be paid, the court
must determine the amount, applying the same principles of damages as
apply in defamation proceedings. For guidance on the proper operation of
the statutory provisions see the very full judgment of Eady J. in *Abu v MGN
Ltd* [2003] 1 W.L.R. 2201, and for the provisions in operation, where the
award of compensation was made also by Eady J. and with further guidance,
see *Cleese v Clark* [2004] E.M.L.R. 3, p.37. Further determinations of compensation by Eady J. have followed. His reduction by 50 per cent of the
amount he would have awarded on a full trial was upheld by the Court of
Appeal in *Nail v News Group Newspapers Ltd* [2005] 1 All E.R. 1040, CA on
the basis that if an unqualified offer to make amends were made and an
agreed apology published, as had happened in the case, there was bound to
be substantial mitigation of the damage. In *Turner v News Group Newspapers
Ltd* [2005] E.M.L.R. 25, p.553 the question of applying the recently established *Burstein* principle (at para.39–063 of the main work) arose and the discount made on the figure that would have been awarded had the dispute gone
to trial was 40 per cent. *Campbell-James v Guardian Media Group plc* [2005]
E.M.L.R. 24, p.542 concerned a libel of the utmost gravity; the discount was
35 per cent.

(3) *Other circumstances*

(iii) Contextual background to the publication

NOTE 6 Add: Another circumstance which, it was held in *Collins Stewart* **39–063**
Ltd v Financial Times Ltd [2005] EWHC 262 (QB), February 25, was not to
be taken into account in aggravation of the damages consisted of further and
later articles published by the defendant newspaper which could also be
defamatory but which were not the subject-matter of complaint. Contrast
para.39–042 of the main text.

CHAPTER 40

ECONOMIC TORTS

I. INTERFERENCE WITH CONTRACTS

(A) INDUCEMENT OF BREACH OF CONTRACT

40–003   NOTE 7: Add at the end: The measure of damages would have been reasonably clear in the unusual circumstances of *OBG Ltd (In Liquidation) v Allan* [2005] 2 W.L.R. 1174, CA had the tort of wilful interference with contractual relations been held to have been committed.

(B) CONSPIRACY

(1) *Pecuniary loss*

40–009   NOTE 42: Add at the end: In *British Midland Tool Ltd v Midland International Tooling Ltd* [2003] 2 B.C.L.C. 523, which concerned a conspiracy against the claimant company by a series of its directors and employees who had set up a competitive business next door, together with a company as a vehicle to carry it on, with the result that the claimant company had to close down, damages for loss of the business, trading losses and closure costs were all claimed as being the result of the unlawful conspiracy; the claimant company was held entitled in principle to have damages assessed under all three heads claimed. See *ibid.*, para.188.

(2) Non-pecuniary loss

NOTE 51: Add at the end: Thus no exemplary damages were awarded in **40–010** *British Midland Tool Ltd v Midland International Tooling Ltd* [2003] 2 B.C.L.C. 523 since the conspiracy was held not to be profit motivated: see *ibid.*, para.252.

II. INJURIOUS FALSEHOOD AND COGNATE TORTS

(A) INJURIOUS FALSEHOOD

2. PASSING OFF

NOTE 15: Add: But this presumption of damage does not run in passing off **40–021** in the absence of deception: *Radio Taxicabs (London) Ltd v Owner Drivers Radio Taxi Services Ltd* [2004] R.P.C. 351, paras 106 to 108.

NOTE 22: Add at the end: The Court of Appeal's doubt in *Reed Executive* **40–022** *plc v Reed Business Information Ltd* [2004] R.P.C. 767, CA as to the appropriateness of awarding damages on the so-called user principle (see para.40–028, n.56, below) was expressed in relation to passing off cases as well as trade mark cases.

NOTE 28: Add at the end: And see *Irvine v Talksport Ltd* [2003] F.S.R. 619, CA where the passing off consisted of the publication of a picture which falsely gave the impression that the claimant racing driver had endorsed the defendant's radio station and the claimant was held entitled to damages based on the amounts charged by him for earlier endorsements of products.

(B) INFRINGEMENT OF RIGHTS IN IMMATERIAL PROPERTY

NOTE 45: Add at the end: In the context of breach of confidence the Court **40–025** of Appeal held that for a variety of reasons a notional licence fee was not the right basis on which to award damages to two film stars for the unauthorised publication of photographs of their wedding: *Douglas v Hello! Ltd (No.8)* [2005] EWCA Civ 595, May 18, at paras 243 to 250.

Insert a new paragraph after para.40–025:

Damages for non-pecuniary loss by way of injured feelings resulting from **40–025A** breach of personal or individual confidence, rather than breach of commercial confidence, have started to appear in recent years. The cases tend to involve breaches by the media, perpetrated against those who are currently referred to as personalities. Thus in *Campbell v MGN Ltd* [2002] E.M.L.R. 30, p.617 the claimant was a well-known fashion model who recovered £2,500 for injured feelings from the publication of unattractive details of her life together with aggravated damages of £1,000; the Court of Appeal reversed on liability and the House of Lords in turn reversed the Court of Appeal stating unanimously that the judge's order be restored. In *Douglas v Hello! Ltd* the claimants who were film stars about to get married and have a very grand wedding were held entitled to damages for distress at the publication of unauthorised photographs but not to aggravated damages: *Douglas v Hello! Ltd (No.5)* [2003] E.M.L.R. 31, p.641 at para.275; the damages were assessed at £3,750 each: *Douglas v Hello! Ltd (No.6)* [2004] E.M.L.R. 2, p.13 at paras 56 and 57 (not challenged in the CA: see *Douglas v Hello! Ltd (No.8)* [2005] EWCA Civ 595, May 18, at para.110). None of the hearings in the Court of Appeal in this extended litigation, now running to eight reported hearings in all, concerned damages other than the last (and then in respect of damages other than the distress damages: see *Douglas v Hello! Ltd (No.8)* [2005] EWCA Civ 595, May 18, at para 6–039, n.40a, and 40–025, n.45, above). The earlier *Cornelius v de Taranto* [2001] E.M.L.R. 12, p.329 did not involve a personality claimant but a teacher who was awarded £3,000 in damages for injured feelings, again for an unauthorised publication and again not appealed on this issue; and *Archer v Williams* [2003] E.M.L.R. 38, p.869 did not involve a media defendant but the claimant's secretary and personal assistant against whom there was awarded for her revelations to the press £2,500.

1. INFRINGEMENT OF TRADE MARKS

40–028   NOTE 56: Add: In *Reed Executive plc v Reed Business Information Ltd* [2004] R.P.C. 767, CA doubt was expressed by the Court of Appeal, at *ibid.*, para.165, about the appropriateness in trade mark cases of awarding damages on the so-called user principle, involving the ascertainment of a reasonable royalty between licensor and licensee, especially where the trade mark concerned is not the sort of mark that is available for hire.

2. INFRINGEMENT OF PATENTS

40–030   Insert a new note after the second sentence of the paragraph:

NOTE 59a: See Aldous L.J.'s extended discussion of damages principles in *SmithKline Beecham plc v Apotex Europe Ltd* [2003] F.S.R. 544, CA where he remarks that, while the normal recovery for a patentee who is not manufacturing is a reasonable royalty, the infringement may cause him a loss exceeding this: *ibid.*, para.8.

3. Infringement of Copyright and Design Right

(1) *In general*

Note 7: Add at the end: And see *London General Holdings Ltd v USP plc* **40–034** [2005] EWCA Civ 931, July 22, where the court had "to consider the very basis upon which damages for breach of copyright are awarded" (*ibid.,* para.26); unauthorised use of the ideas contained in the copyrighted material, as opposed to unauthorised use of the material itself, was not enough: see the discussion at *ibid.,* paras 29 to 36.

Add at the end of the paragraph: In *Peninsular Business Services Ltd v* **40–036** *Citation plc* [2004] F.S.R. 359 claimant and defendant were in the business of providing certain consulting services, the primary means of obtaining business being by the canvassing of clients. In setting up the business various manuals were used and in breach of contract the defendant copied materials from the claimant's manuals to their own manuals. The claim for lost profits to the claimant's business failed because, although the infringing material had been used in competition with that business and was a central feature in setting up the system of business, it played no part in the selling of the claimant's services which occurred through the normal process of competition by the canvassing of clients for which purpose the material was not required. Instead, the provision of the documents being required for the businesses, the court awarded simply the cost to the defendant of producing or commissioning a non-infringing set of materials. To the extent that this award was based on benefit to the defendant rather than loss to the claimant it has restitutionary overtones along the lines of the cases considered at para.12–002 *et seq.* of the main text.

(2) *The provision for additional damages*

Note 29: Add at the end: As to the meaning of flagrancy see *Dyson Ltd v* **40–038** *Qualtex (UK) Ltd* [2005] R.P.C. 395, paras 338 to 343.

(b) Relation with exemplary damages

Insert a new note at the end of the paragraph: **40–040**

Note 52a: Nevertheless Gray J. in *Collins Stewart Ltd v Financial Times Ltd* [2005] EWHC 262 (QB), February 25, tended to the view that additional damages under s.97(2) are akin to exemplary damages because, if they were merely aggravated damages, it would be difficult to justify their being awarded to corporate claimants which seems to be commonly done in breach of copyright cases: *ibid.,* para.33. This is indeed a difficulty; the appropriateness of allowing the additional damages for corporate claimants does not appear to have been specifically addressed to date. See also at para.3–011, n.44, above

(c) Criteria for assessment

40–041   NOTE 65: Add at the end: Nor was flagrancy for the purposes of additional damages shown in *Fraser-Woodward Ltd v British Broadcasting Corporation Brighter Pictures Ltd* [2005] E.M.L.R. 22, p.487: see at paras 89 to 91.

CHAPTER 41

MISREPRESENTATION

I. FRAUDULENT MISREPRESENTATION: DECEIT

1. THE TORTIOUS MEASURE OF DAMAGES

Add at the end of the paragraph: *Clef Aquitaine* is explored further in **41–006** *Black v Davies* [2005] EWCA Civ 531, May 6. From that decision it would seem to follow that compound interest will not be awarded on damages awarded in an action of deceit and will be confined to available claims for equitable compensation based on fraud, and then only where the fraudster has obtained and retained money or other benefits which was not the case in *Black v Davies* itself. The decision is examined at para.15–019, n.88, above.

2. HEADS OF DAMAGE

(1) *Pecuniary loss*

(a) Where the claimant has contracted to buy shares

(i) Normal measure

Insert a new paragraph after para.41–015:

Halston Holdings SA v Simons [2005] EWHC 30 (QB), January 21, is a fur- **41–015A** ther interesting case on damages for deceit in inducing the purchase of shares, reflecting the principles appearing at paras 41–013 to 41–015 of the main text. The claimant bought shares in a company relying on the defendant's false and fraudulent certificate of the level of inter-group indebtedness included in the assets of the company, the level given being about £1 million lower than its actual level. A year after the purchase the company collapsed and went into administration. Had the certificate not been signed and produced the claimant would not have entered into or completed the agreement to purchase and would not have lost all of its investment. The damages awarded for the loss on the shares represented their full purchase price without any deduction, since the shares had no real value at the time of the purchase and the claimant had had no opportunity to realise its investment before the company's collapse. Like the horse which has a latent disease when sold and later dies (in the instructive illustration in *Twycross v Grant* cited in *Halston* at para.85), the company which collapsed was already ill at the time of the purchase of the shares by the claimant: see *Halston* at para.93 and the whole discussion of damages at *ibid.*, paras 84 to 97.

II. NEGLIGENT MISREPRESENTATION

2. THE TORTIOUS MEASURE OF DAMAGES

41–046   Add a new note at the end of the paragraph:

NOTE 28a: *Royscot* continues to trouble the law, with statements such as that in *Peekay Intermark Ltd v Australian and New Zealand Banking Group Ltd* [2005] EWHC 830 (Comm), May 25, that the claimant, suing under s.2(1) of the 1967 Act, "was entitled in accordance with ... [*Royscot*] ... to the fraud measure of damages" (para.69). In that particular case (at para.41–049, below) there was probably no difference between the liability in fraud and the liability in negligence.

3. HEADS OF DAMAGE

(1) *Pecuniary loss*

(a) Where there is a contract

(i) Normal measure

41–049   Add at the end of the paragraph: *Peekay Intermark Ltd v Australian and New Zealand Banking Group Ltd* [2005] EWHC 830 (Comm), May 25, was concerned with the mis-selling of an emerging markets investment product, marketed by the defendant, into which the claimant invested 250,000 dollars. Had it known the true nature of the investment it would not have bought but, having bought, it was locked into the investment for some time, eventually realising it for some 6,000 dollars. In its claim under s.2(1) of the Misrepresentation Act 1967 the claimant was awarded the difference between the sum invested and the amount ultimately realised.

BOOK TWO
PART THREE
HUMAN RIGHTS

CHAPTER 42

DAMAGES UNDER THE HUMAN RIGHTS ACT

1. INTRODUCTION

Insert a new paragraph after para. 42–003:

In *R. (on the application of Greenfield) v Secretary of State for the Home* **42–003A**
Department [2005] 1 W.L.R. 673, HL, the House of Lords considered the
relationship between the cause of action under the HRA and the attitude
towards similar claims taken by the ECHR. Lord Bingham, delivering the
judgment of the court, pointed out that the action under the HRA is very different from an ordinary action for damages in the domestic courts because,
by virtue of the UK's treaty obligations, the expectation is that where a Member State is found to have violated the Convention, it will act promptly to prevent a repetition, thereby serving the Convention's primary object. The
provision of affording "just satisfaction" to the injured party is thus per-
ceived to be a secondary object. In deciding whether to award damages, the
domestic court must be satisfied as to four preconditions:

(1) that a finding of unlawfulness or prospective unlawfulness is made,
based on breach or prospective breach by a public authority of a
Convention right;
(2) the court has power to award damages in civil proceedings;
(3) the court is satisfied that an award of damages is necessary to afford
"just satisfaction" to the victim; and
(4) the court considers that an award of damages is just and appropriate.

Lord Bingham then said (at para.6):

"It would seem to be clear that a domestic court may not award damages
unless satisfied that it is necessary to do so, but if satisfied that it is necessary to do so it is hard to see how the court could consider it other
than just and appropriate to do so. In deciding whether to award
damages, and if so how much, the court is not strictly bound by the

principles applied by the [ECHR] in awarding compensation under Article 41 of the Convention, but it must take those principles into account. It is therefore to Strasbourg that British Courts must look for guidance on the award of damages."

It can fairly be said that this case is now the leading authority on the award of damages under the HRA, particularly in relation to allegations of breach of Article 6.

42–005   Add at the end of the paragraph:

In *R. (on the application of Greenfield) v Secretary of State for the Home Department* [2005] 1 W.L.R. 673, HL (February 16, 2005), the House of Lords rejected the notion that the HRA is a "tort statute". Lord Bingham said (at para.19):

"The 1998 Act is not a tort statute. Its objects are different and broader. Even in a case where a finding of a violation is not judged to afford the applicant just satisfaction, such a finding will be an important part of his remedy and an important vindication of the right he has asserted. Damages need not ordinarily be awarded to encourage high standards of compliance by member states, since they are already bound in international law to perform their duties under the Convention in good faith, although it may be different if there is felt to be a need to encourage compliance by individual officials or classes of official. Secondly, the purpose of incorporating the Convention in domestic law through the 1998 Act was not to give victims better remedies at home than they could secure in Strasbourg but to give them the same remedies without the delay and expense of resort to Strasbourg. . . . Thirdly, section 8(4) requires a domestic court to take into account the principles applied by the European Court under article 41 not only in determining whether to award damages but also in determining the amount of an award. There could be no clearer indication that courts in this country should look to Strasbourg and not to domestic precedents."

2. SCOPE OF THE CAUSE OF ACTION

Insert new paragraphs after para.42–006:

42–006A   The scope of the cause of action under s.6(1) was considered by the House of Lords in *Re McKerr* [2004] 1 W.L.R. 807, HL, where it was held that s.6(1) only applies to unlawful killings (within the context of a breach of Article 2, the Right to Life) after the HRA came into force on October 2, 2000, but not ones occurring before that date. This was an application of the general rule that the HRA is not retrospective. In respect of the Right to Life, the principle was also applied to the State's obligation to hold an investigation into unlawful killings, even though that might be a continuing obligation. Thus, the foundation for that obligation was the unlawful death, and for the applicant to have jurisdiction to bring proceedings for judicial review in respect of the UK's failure to hold an adequate investigation, it was necessary for the death to have occurred after October 2, 2000. Thus Lord Nicholls said:

> "Having had the advantage of much fuller arguments I respectfully consider that some of these courts, including the Divisional Court in *Hurst's* case and the Court of Appeal in *Khan's* case, fell into error by failing to keep clearly in mind the distinction between (1) rights arising under the Convention and (2) rights created by the 1998 Act by reference to the Convention. These two sets of rights now exist side by side. But there are significant differences between them. The former existed before the enactment of the 1998 Act and they continue to exist. They are not as such part of this country's law because the Convention does not form part of this country's law. That is still the position. These rights, arising under the Convention, are to be contrasted with rights created by the 1998 Act. The latter came into existence for the first time on 2 October 2000. They are part of this country's law. The extent of these rights, created as they were by the 1998 Act, depends upon the proper interpretation of that Act. It by no means follows that the continuing existence of a right arising under the Convention in respect of an act occurring before the 1998 Act came into force will be mirrored by a corresponding right created by the 1998 Act. Whether it finds reflection in this way in the 1998 Act depends upon the proper interpretation of the 1998 Act."

The House of Lords also considered, *obiter*, the position if the death had in fact occurred after October 2, 2000 and the fact that the claimant had been awarded £10,000 by the ECHR. On this basis, it was held that he would still have had jurisdiction to bring proceedings for judicial review if he was still not in the position intended to have been achieved by the fulfilment of the State's obligation to hold an investigation into his father's death. Thus, the government's obligation to comply with the ECHR is a continuing one, and one can contemplate successive actions for damages where, despite a finding of non-compliance, the government continues to fail to fulfil its obligations. However, the House of Lords rejected the suggestion of a new common law right to an effective investigation into death, this being an area governed by statute and therefore inappropriate for common law intervention.

The scope of the cause of action was further considered in *A v Head* **42–006B** *Teacher and Governors of Lord Grey School* [2004] Q.B. 1231, CA, where the claimant had been unlawfully excluded from school and a claim was brought in damages for breach of Article 2 of the First Protocol which provides:

> "*Right to Education*. No person shall be denied the right to education. In the exercise of any functions which it assumes in relation to education and to teaching, the state shall respect the right of parents to ensure such education and teaching in conformity with their own religious and philosophical convictions."

In the course of his judgment, Sedley L.J., giving the judgment of the court said:

> "For A, Miss Booth QC submitted . . . that the Convention right to education is not fixed in content but takes the form of the provision made by each member state. Exclusion pursuant to law, provided the law itself does not breach the Convention, therefore involves no denial of the Convention right. It does not follow that every unlawful exclusion does amount to a breach: for example a temporary failure to provide transport when the law requires it will not amount to a denial of the right to education. Nor does it follow that no lawful act can amount to a breach: excluding a child for refusing to submit to corporal punishment which itself breaches the Convention, or exercising a legal power, if there were one, to exclude a child permanently from all access to education, would create an incompatibility between domestic law and the Convention and attract one or other of the remedies afforded by the Human Rights Act 1998. But between these extremes, Ms Booth submitted, lie cases like the present in which an unlawful exclusion has brought about a direct denial of access to the education provided for in the statute law of England and Wales, in the literal sense that A was for ten months not permitted to attend a school or given appropriate education by other means. All else goes, if to anything, to the quantum of damage."

Accepting these submissions, Sedley L.J. said:

> "The realistic principle that, subject to the Convention's own limits, the right to education takes the form prescribed in each member state carries, in my judgment, the necessary corollary that any question whether there has been a violation of the right has to be answered initially in terms of the applicable domestic law. For the reasons given by Ms Booth, which I accept, the answer yielded by the latter will not be determinative, but it is the indispensable starting point. Thus if no breach of domestic law is found, it is only if that law itself materially offends against the Convention that the Human Rights Act 1998 moves one on to the question of a remedy. If a breach of domestic law is found, it remains to be decided whether it has resulted in a denial of the Convention right. Put broadly, there will be such a denial where the breach of domestic law has resulted in the pupil's being unable to avail himself of the means of education which presently exist in England and Wales-not, for example, by being temporarily unable to reach the school premises for want of transport, but by being shut out for a significant or an indefinite period from access to such education as the law provides for him or her."

(1) Who can be sued

Insert a new note at the end of the paragraph:

NOTE 22a: There is a close analogy between the question whether a private body is exercising a public function for the purposes of the HRA and the question which arises in the field of public law whether a body is exercising public law functions so as to be amenable to judicial review. Thus, in *Poplar Housing and Regeneration Community Association Ltd v Donoghue* [2001] 4 All E.R. 604, where the issue was whether the bodies whose decisions were the subject of challenge were public authorities within the meaning of s.6 of the HRA, Lord Woolf pointed out at para.65(i) of the judgment of the court that s.6 "is clearly inspired by the approach developed by the courts in identifying the bodies and activities subject to judicial review. See also *R (Heather) v Leonard Cheshire Foundation and another* [2002] EWCA Civ 366; [2002] 2 All E.R. 936". In *Hampshire CC v Beer (t/a Hammer Trout Farm)* [2003] EWCA Civ 1056, Dyson L.J., referring to Lord Woolf's dictum, said:

> "No doubt for this reason, it was common ground in oral argument before us that (i) the tests for a functional public authority within the meaning of section 6(3)(b) and for amenability to judicial review are, for practical purposes, the same, and (ii) the observations in both *Donoghue* and *Heather* are equally relevant to the application of both tests."

In *X v Y:* [2004] EWCA Civ 662 the Court of Appeal considered the effect of the HRA on existing legislation and stated that the effect of s.6 in a case involving a claim against a private employer was to reinforce the strong interpretative obligation imposed on the tribunal by s.3. The effect of s.3 on the interpretation of s.98 of Employment Rights Act was best described as oblique rather than as directly or indirectly horizontal. By a process of interpretation the Article 8 right was blended with the law on unfair dismissal given in ERA, but without creating new private law causes of action against private law employers.

3. CRITERIA FOR DECISION WHETHER TO AWARD DAMAGES

(1) Interaction of sections 8(3) and 8(4)

Add at the end of the paragraph:

In *R. (on the application of Greenfield) v Secretary of State for the Home Department* [2005] 1 W.L.R. 673, HL, Lord Bingham considered that s.8(4) could provide no clearer indication that the domestic courts should look to Strasbourg and not to domestic precedents, not only in determining whether to award damages at all, but also in determining the amount of the award.

Insert a new paragraph after para.42–025:

42–025A   The approach of the court to a claim for damages under the HRA, and the relevance of the Strasbourg jurisprudence, was considered by the Court of Appeal in *Anufrijeva & anr v London Borough of Southwark; R. (on the application of N) v Secretary of State for the Home Department; R. (on the application of M) v Secretary of State for the Home Department* [2004] Q.B. 1124, CA. Giving the judgment of the court, Lord Woolf L.C.J. said at paras 52 and 53:

> "The sections of the HRA . . . establish a code governing the award of damages which has to be applied with due regard to the Strasbourg jurisprudence. However, as we shall show, the assistance to be derived from that jurisprudence is limited. The remedy of damages generally plays a less prominent role in actions based on breaches of the articles of the ECHR, than in actions based on breaches of private law obligations where, more often than not, the only remedy claimed is damages. Where an infringement of an individual's human rights has occurred, the concern will usually be to bring the infringement to an end and any question of compensation will be of secondary, if any, importance. This is reflected in the fact that, when it is necessary to resort to the courts to uphold and protect human rights, the remedies that are most frequently sought are the orders which are the descendants of the historic prerogative orders or declaratory judgments."

The court emphasised the following five points:

(1)   the award of damages under the HRA is confined to the class of unlawful acts of public authorities identified by s.6(1);

(2)   the court has a discretion as to whether to make an award (it must be "just and appropriate" to do so) by contrast to the position in relation to common law claims where there is a right to damages;

(3)   the award must be necessary to achieve "just satisfaction", using language that is distinct from the approach at common law where a claimant is invariably entitled, so far as money can achieve this, to be restored to the position he would have been in if he had not suffered the injury of which complaint is made;

(4)   the court is required to take into account in determining whether damages are payable and the amount of damages payable the different principles applied by the ECHR in awarding compensation; and

(5)   exemplary damages are not awarded.

42–026   Add at the end of the paragraph:

See, however, *R. (on the application of Greenfield) v Secretary of State for the Home Department* [2005] 1 W.L.R. 673, HL, at paras 18 and 19.

42–027   Add at the end of the paragraph:

It seems clear that, as a result of the decision of the House of Lords in *R. (on the application of Greenfield) v Secretary of State for the Home*

Department [2005] 1 W.L.R. 673, HL, the domestic courts will not be bucking the general trend and that there will be a tendency, particularly in cases of violation of Article 6, to decide that the mere finding of violation is sufficient just satisfaction and that no award of damages or compensation is necessary.

Delete the words from "However, it could be argued that there is, in fact, a   **42–028**
significant difference . . ." to the end of the paragraph and substitute: That this is the case has been confirmed by the House of Lords in *R. (on the application of Greenfield) v Secretary of State for the Home Department* [2005] 1 W.L.R. 673, HL: see *per* Lord Bingham at paras 18 and 19.

Insert a new note at the end of the paragraph: **42–030**

NOTE 54a: In *Anufrijeva & anr v London Borough of Southwark; R. (on the application of N) v Secretary of State for the Home Department; R. (on the application of M) v Secretary of State for the Home Department* [2004] Q.B. 1124, CA, Stanley Burton J.'s judgment in *R. (KB) v Mental Health Review Tribunal* was described by the Court of Appeal as impressive and the quality of the judgment was commended. And see also *R. (on the application of Greenfield) v Secretary of State for the Home Department* [2005] 1 W.L.R. 673, HL.

(2) Manner of breach

Insert a new note at the end of the paragraph: **42–031**

NOTE 57a: Contrary to the above-expressed view, however, the Court of Appeal in *Anufrijeva & anr v London Borough of Southwark; R. (on the application of N) v Secretary of State for the Home Department; R. (on the application of M) v Secretary of State for the Home Department* [2004] Q.B. 1124, CA, stated that the scale and manner of a violation of the Convention can be taken into account, citing *Halford* as an instance of the ECHR being led to award damages by the seriousness of the manner and way in which the violation of the Convention had taken place.

(3) Substantive or procedural breach

Add at the end of the paragraph: **42–032**

In *R. (on the application of Greenfield) v Secretary of State for the Home Department* [2005] 1 W.L.R. 673, HL, Lord Bingham, at para. 16, cited the Grand Chamber of the ECHR in *Kingsley v United Kingdom* (2002) 35 E.H.R.R. 177 where they said:

"In all the circumstances, and in accordance with its normal practice, in civil and criminal cases, as regards violations of article 6(1) caused by failures of objective and structural independence and impartiality, the court does not consider it appropriate to award monetary compensation to the applicant in respect of loss of procedural opportunity or distress, loss or damage allegedly flowing from the outcome of the domestic proceedings."

Lord Bingham then stated: "Thus, whatever the practice in other classes of case, the ordinary practice is not to make an award in cases of structural bias."

4. THE COURT'S APPROACH TO DETERMINING *QUANTUM*

42–038   Add at the end of the paragraph:

In *R. (on the application of Greenfield) v Secretary of State for the Home Department* [2005] 1 W.L.R. 673, HL, Lord Bingham stated at para.19 that s.8(4) could give no clearer indication that, in determining the *quantum* of an award, the courts should look to Strasbourg and not to domestic precedents. At first sight, this might appear to be a strong endorsement of the second possible approach. However, Lord Bingham did not address the situation where there are no principles or no clear principles, or where, as is often the case, the Strasbourg precedents are inconsistent with each other. Lord Bingham said that the domestic courts "are not inflexibly bound by Strasbourg awards in what may be different cases. But they should not aim to be significantly more or less generous than the court might be expected to be, in a case where it was willing to make an award at all." It is submitted that this is consistent with the approach advocated below at paragraph 42–039.

42–043   Add at the end of the paragraph:

In so far as Lord Woolf's principles are, and were intended to be, a statement of the principles of the ECHR in its approach to the *quantum* of damages, it can now be stated that these principles represent domestic law in relation to the approach of the domestic courts to *quantum* in awarding damages under the HRA. This is because the ECHR's principles were firmly laid down as the basis for such awards by the House of Lords in *R. (on the application of Greenfield) v Secretary of State for the Home Department* [2005] 1 W.L.R. 673, HL. Thus, Lord Bingham rejected the submission that domestic courts should simply apply domestic scales of damages and should feel free to depart from the scale of damages awarded by the ECHR. He said (at para.19) that it is to Strasbourg that domestic courts should turn under the HRA for three reasons:

(1) the HRA is not a tort statute but has different and broader objects;
(2) the rationale behind the HRA is to give victims the same remedies in the domestic courts as they would have in the ECHR, but with less delay and expense; and

(3) the provisions of s.8(4) require a domestic court to take into account the principles of the ECHR when making awards of damages under Article 41, including in determining the *quantum*.

In the light of these factors, Lord Bingham said: "[Domestic courts] are not inflexibly bound by Strasbourg awards in what may be different cases. But they should not aim to be significantly more or less generous than the court might be expected to be, in a case where it was willing to make an award at all."

Insert a new paragraph after para.42–043:

In *Anufrijeva & anr v London Borough of Southwark; R. (on the application of N) v Secretary of State for the Home Department; R. (on the application of M) v Secretary of State for the Home Department* [2004] Q.B. 1124, CA, the Court of Appeal considered the correct approach towards determining *quantum* where the breach arises from maladministration. The case, which comprised three consolidated appeals, had the following features in common: each involved a claimant who came to the UK seeking asylum; each claimant was complaining of a failure by the Home Office to comply with its statutory duty whereby the claimants were entitled to receive benefits or advantages; finally, that failure was due to maladministration which constituted a breach of Article 8 of the Convention. In relation to the approach to the *quantum* of damages, the court stated at paras 74 to 76:

42–043A

"Where, however, in a claim under the HRA, the court decides that it is appropriate to award damages, the levels of damages awarded in respect of torts as reflected in the guidelines issued by the Judicial Studies Board, the levels of awards made by the Criminal Injuries Compensation Board and by the Parliamentary Ombudsman and the Local Government Ombudsman may all provide some rough guidance where the consequences of the infringement of human rights are similar to that being considered in the comparator selected. In cases of maladministration where the consequences are not of a type which gives rise to any right to compensation under our civil law, the awards of the Ombudsman may be the only comparator.

We have indicated that a finding of a breach of a positive obligation under article 8 to provide support will be rare, and will be likely to occur only where this impacts severely on family life. Where such a breach does occur, it is unlikely that there will be any ready comparator to assist in the assessment of damages. There are good reasons why, where the breach arises from maladministration, in those cases where an award of damages is appropriate, the scale of such damages should be modest. The cost of supporting those in need falls on society as a whole. Resources are limited and payments of substantial damages will deplete the resources available for other needs of the public including primary care. If the impression is created that asylum seekers whether genuine or not are profiting from their status, this could bring the Human Rights Act into disrepute.

Similar considerations apply to delay in processing asylum claims or the procedure for admitting the relatives of refugees. Those admitted are likely, at least initially, to require support. In view of the numbers involved, some delay in the processing of asylum claims is inevitable and, at times, in the interest of the asylum seekers themselves, the process is understandably lengthy. The factors that weigh against recognising administrative delay as engaging article 8 militate equally in favour of either no award or modest awards where article 8 is engaged."

5. PARTICULAR ASPECTS OF *QUANTUM*

(1) Causation

Insert a new paragraph after para.42–044:

42–044A   The same principle was applied in *Kingsley v United Kingdom* (2002) 35 E.H.R.R. 177 where the Grand Chamber of the ECHR stated, at para.40:

"The court recalls that it is well established that the principle underlying the provision of just satisfaction for a breach of Article 6 is that the applicant should as far as possible be put in the position he would have enjoyed had the proceedings complied with the Convention's requirements. The court will award monetary compensation under Article 41 only where it is satisfied that the loss or damage complained of was actually caused by the violation it has found, since the State cannot be required to pay damages in respect of losses for which it is not responsible."

In *R. (on the application of Greenfield) v Secretary of State for the Home Department* [2005] 1 W.L.R. 673, HL, this passage was adopted by Lord Bingham as applying to a claim for damages for breach of Article 6 in the domestic courts. He said at para.11:

"As appears from the passage just cited, the court has ordinarily been willing to depart from its practice of finding a violation of article 6 to be, in itself, just satisfaction under article 41 only where the court finds a causal connection between the violation found and the loss for which an applicant claims to be compensated."

(2) Non-pecuniary loss

42–045   Add at the end of the paragraph:

As the House of Lords made clear in *R. (on the application of Greenfield) v Secretary of State for the Home Department* [2005] 1 W.L.R. 673, HL, though, the ordinary practice is not to make an award for non-pecuniary loss in cases of "structural bias", namely "violations of article 6(1) caused by failure of objective or structural independence and impartiality" (see *Kingsley v United Kingdom* (2002) 35 E.H.R.R. 177 at para.43, cited by Lord Bingham in *Greenfield* at para.16).

(3) Loss of a chance

Insert a new paragraph after para.42–049:

The jurisprudence of the ECHR in relation to the award of damages for lost opportunity was considered by the House of Lords in *R. (on the application of Greenfield) v Secretary of State for the Home Department* [2005] 1 W.L.R. 673, HL, at paras 12 to 14 of the judgment of the court given by Lord Bingham. He concluded: **42–049A**

> "Thus while the court laid down in the authoritative case of *Kingsley* [at para.42–044A above] in the passage quoted in para 10 above, and repeated in *Edwards and Lewis v United Kingdom* 27 October 2004, paras 46 and 49, that the court will award monetary compensation under article 41 only where it is satisfied that the loss or damage complained of was actually caused by the violation it has found, and it has repeatedly stressed that it will not speculate on what the outcome of the proceedings would have been but for the violation, it has on occasion been willing in appropriate cases to make an award if of opinion that the applicant has been deprived of a real chance of a better outcome."

See also *Hooper v United Kingdom* (2005) 41 E.H.R.R. 1, considered below at para.42–069C, where Mance J. (as he then was) had assessed that, but for breach of Article 6, the magistrate "might well have been persuaded to a different result if the applicant's counsel had been able to make representations concerning the order". The ECHR said that while this conclusion was not expressed in such strong terms as in, for example, *Perks v United Kingdom*, the court "considers that it is sufficient to support the applicant's claim that he suffered some loss of opportunity due to the breach in this case" and the applicant was awarded €8,000.

Add at the end of the paragraph: **42–052**

See further the decision of the House of Lords in *R. (on the application of Greenfield) v Secretary of State for the Home Department* [2005] 1 W.L.R. 673, HL, particularly *per* Lord Bingham at para.16 where *Kingsley v United Kingdom* (2002) 35 E.H.R.R. 177 was cited and adopted.

6. DAMAGES UNDER PARTICULAR CONVENTION ARTICLES

(4) Article 6: Right to a Fair Trial

Insert new paragraphs after para.42–069:

42–069A The scope of the domestic courts to make awards of damages for violation of Article 6 was considered, and significantly limited, by the House of Lords in *R. (on the application of Greenfield) v Secretary of State for the Home Department* [2005] 1 W.L.R. 673, HL. Lord Bingham, giving the judgment of the court, said that, in general, a finding of violation of Article 6 will be sufficient "just satisfaction" and that this is a principle which clearly underlies the jurisprudence of the ECHR. Whether an award will be made will depend on the requirements of justice in the individual case and the strength of the case in relation to proof of causation. However "the ordinary practice is not to make an award in cases of structural bias" (*per* Lord Bingham at para.16). He said that the pursuit of damages should rarely if ever be an end in itself in an Article 6 case (para.30). Even in the rare case where a court is persuaded that an award of damages for violation of Article 6(1) is appropriate, it was made clear that the quantum will be modest and will not necessarily follow domestic tariffs. Lord Bingham said that the domestic courts "are not inflexibly bound by Strasbourg awards in what may be different cases. But they should not aim to be significantly more or less generous than the court might be expected to be, in a case where it was willing to make an award at all" (para.19).

42–069B In *Connors v United Kingdom* (2005) 40 E.H.R.R. 9, the ECHR found that there had been a breach of Article 8 alone where the applicant and his family, who were gypsies, were evicted from a site run by the local authority without being given the opportunity to challenge in a court the allegations made against him and his family. It was held that the power to evict without the burden of giving reasons liable to be examined as to their merits by an independent tribunal did not respond to any specific goal or provide any specific benefit to members of the gypsy community. Accordingly the eviction of the applicant and his family was not attended "by the requisite procedural safeguards, namely the requirement to establish proper justification for the serious interference with his rights, and consequently could not be regarded as justified". The reference to the requisite procedural safeguards and the opportunity for the merits of the decision to be examined by an independent tribunal shows that, although the decision was only of violation of Article 8, this was, in reality, a combined breach of Article 6(1) and Article 8. The ECHR concluded that the applicant suffered non-pecuniary damage through feelings of frustration and injustice, that the finding of violation was not sufficient compensation, and they awarded him €14,000.

42–069C A recent case in which the ECHR awarded damages to a British applicant for breach of Article 6 alone is *Hooper v United Kingdom* (2005) 41 E.H.R.R. 1

where the applicant, after making a disturbance in the magistrates' court, had been summarily bound over to keep the peace with 28 days' imprisonment in default of his own recognisance and/or a suitable surety. Neither the applicant nor his lawyer was given any opportunity to make representations about the terms of the order, and in the event he was imprisoned for 14 days. The ECHR found that there had been violations of Article 6(1) and 6(3) and awarded the applicant €8,000 for non-pecuniary damage. The applicant had claimed £10,000 for the detention and an additional £1,000 for "the distress caused by the failure of the court to hear him in his defence". So far as causation is concerned, the ECHR referred to the fact that Mance J. (as he then was) assessed that the magistrate "might well have been persuaded to a different result if the applicant's counsel had been able to make representations concerning the order". The ECHR said that while this conclusion was not expressed in such strong terms as in, for example, *Perks v United Kingdom*, it "considers that it is sufficient to support the applicant's claim that he suffered some loss of opportunity due to the breach in this case."

(5) Article 8: Right to Respect for Private and Family Life

Insert in the text after the quotation from *Campbell v Mirror Group*   **42–072**
Newspapers Ltd: The decision of the Court of Appeal to disallow the claimant's claim for damages was overturned by the House of Lords ([2004] UKHL 22, May 6) where their Lordships referred to the balancing exercise to be carried out. Thus, Lord Hope of Craighead said at *ibid.*, paras 104 and 105:

> "In my opinion the Court of Appeal's approach is open to the criticism that, because they wrongly held that these details were not entitled to protection under the law of confidence, they failed to carry out the required balancing exercise.
>
> The context for this exercise is provided by articles 8 and 10 of the Convention. The rights guaranteed by these articles are qualified rights. Article 8(1) protects the right to respect for private life, but recognition is given in article 8(2) to the protection of the rights and freedoms of others. Article 10(1) protects the right to freedom of expression, but article 10(2) recognises the need to protect the rights and freedoms of others. The effect of these provisions is that the right to privacy which lies at the heart of an action for breach of confidence has to be balanced against the right of the media to impart information to the public. And the right of the media to impart information to the public has to be balanced in its turn against the respect that must be given to private life."

At first instance, Morland J. had awarded Naomi Campbell the sum of £2,500 for the breach of her Article 8 rights and this award was restored by the House of Lords. In the Court of Appeal, Lord Phillips M.R. had said that the sum was modest for a particular reason (see [2003] 1 All E.R. 224, CA, at 228): it had been conceded from the outset that the newspaper had been entitled to publish the fact that she was a drug addict and was receiving treatment for her addiction. The claim for damages related only to the additional information conveyed by the articles and the photographs published.

Insert new paragraphs after para. 42–073:

42–073A   Claims for damages under Article 8 came before the Court of Appeal in the case of *Anufrijeva & anr v London Borough of Southwark; R. (on the application of N) v Secretary of State for the Home Department; R. (on the application of M) v Secretary of State for the Home Department* [2004] Q.B. 1124, CA. The Court of Appeal took this opportunity to consider in detail the power of the courts to award damages for breach of the Convention and how that power should be exercised. The court concluded that Sullivan J. had been correct to accept that Article 8 is capable of imposing on a State a positive obligation to provide support, but they continued:

> "We find it hard to conceive, however, of a situation in which the predicament of an individual will be such that Article 8 requires him to be provided with welfare support, where his predicament is not sufficiently severe to engage Article 3. Article 8 may more readily be engaged where a family unit is involved. Where the welfare of children is at stake, Article 8 may require the provision of welfare support in a manner which enables family life to continue."

The Court of Appeal next considered the circumstances in which maladministration will be found to have constituted a breach of Article 8. It was held that before inaction can amount to a lack of respect of private and family life, there must be an element of culpability, and at least a knowledge that the claimant's private and family life are at risk. Where the complaint is of delay, the approach of the ECHR and the Commission was endorsed, exemplified by two particular cases. Thus, in *H v United Kingdom* (1988) 10 E.H.R.R. 95 Article 8 was held by the ECHR to have been infringed by delay in the conduct of access and adoption proceedings because the proceedings "lay within an area in which procedural delay may lead to a de facto determination of the matter in issue". However, in *Askar v United Kingdom* (Application No.26373/95) the Commission held the application to be inadmissible where the complaint was of substantial delay in granting the claimant (a refugee) permission for his family to join him in this country when the claimant had not seen his family for at least six years, stating: "it is not apparent that the delay in the proceedings has had any prejudicial effect on their eventual determination". It would thus appear that, to be successful, it is likely to be necessary to show that the delay has had a substantive effect on the outcome. The Court of Appeal also emphasised the need to have regard to resources when considering the obligations imposed upon the State, and they concluded that maladministration will only infringe Article 8 where the consequence is serious.

Having considered when in principle damages should be awarded and the **42–073C** correct approach to the assessment of damages, the Court of Appeal in *Anufrijeva* then considered each of the individual appeals before it. In the event, none of the applicants was actually successful.

In a different context, in *Wainwright v Home Office* [2004] 2 A.C. 406 Lord **42–073D** Hoffmann said at *ibid.*, para.51:

> "Article 8 may justify a monetary remedy for an intentional invasion of privacy by a public authority, even if no damage is suffered other than distress for which damages are not ordinarily recoverable. It does not follow that a merely negligent act should, contrary to general principle, give rise to a claim for damages for distress because it affects privacy rather than some other interest like bodily safety: compare *Hicks v Chief Constable of the South Yorkshire Police* [1992] 2 All E.R. 65."

Add at the end of the paragraph: The appeal by Thames Water Utilities to **42–074** the House of Lords was allowed (see [2004] 2 A.C. 42) when it was held that the claim under the 1998 Act was ill-founded and the scheme set up by the 1991 Act complied with M's Convention rights. It was decided that the Convention did not accord absolute protection to property or even to residential premises. It required a fair balance to be struck between the interests of persons whose homes and property were affected and the interests of customers and the general public.

Insert new paragraphs after para.42–075:

A further area in which it is thought that the provisions of Article 8 may **42–075A** have an impact is in relation to care expenses for brain-damaged children, and in particular whether such expenses should be assessed on the basis of residential accommodation provided by the local authority or of independent living at home: see *Sowden v Lodge* [2005] 1 W.L.R. 2129, CA. Section 23(8) of the Children Act 1989 provides: "Where a local authority provide accommodation for a child whom they are looking after and who is disabled, they shall, so far as is reasonably practicable, secure that the accommodation is not unsuitable to his particular needs." This section was considered by Peter Gibson L.J. in *R. v Brent LBC ex p. S* [1994] 1 F.L.R. 203 in which he analysed the obligations of s.23(8) in the following terms:

> "The wording of the duty in section 23(8) seems to me designed to avoid placing an unrealistically heavy burden on local authorities. The accommodation to be secured is not required to be suitable to the particular needs of the child but only to be not unsuitable, and the duty to secure even that is qualified by what is reasonably practicable. Accordingly, it may not be reasonably practicable to secure accommodation which is not unsuitable, but so long as the council is doing the best it can, within the bounds of what is reasonably practicable, to secure not unsuitable accommodation, I do not think it is in breach of its statutory duty."

This decision pre-dated the coming into force of the HRA and it is now arguable that this interpretation of the local authority's obligation is no longer good law if it would enable them to provide a quality of accommodation and care which is inferior to the standard that might be expected from what is reasonable, as to do so would constitute a breach of Article 8: see *Batantu v LB of Islington* [2000] 4 CCLR 445, *R v A* [2000] UKHL 25 and *Bouamar v Belgium* [1988] ECHR 9106/80. If such an interpretation is correct, then a defendant could argue, in a case involving a brain-damaged child, that the child's interests are sufficiently protected by the local authority's obligations under the 1989 Act, as interpreted in the light of Article 8, so that it is not necessary to provide for a more expensive regime enabling the child to live independently at home.

42–075B   Although claims under Article 8 have been relatively unsuccessful in the domestic courts within the regime of the HRA, British applicants continue to find success in Strasbourg. An example is *Connors v United Kingdom* (2005) 40 E.H.R.R. 9 where the ECHR awarded the applicant €14,000 for breach of Article 8 where he and his family had been evicted from a gypsy site run by the local authority without being given the opportunity to challenge in a court the allegations made against him and his family. Although there was a finding of violation of Article 8 alone, this was, in reality, a breach of both Articles 6 and Article 8. See further para.42–069B above. It is of some interest that in *Leeds City Council v Price* [2005] 3 All E.R. 573, CA, the Court of Appeal found that the decision of the ECHR in *Connors* was inconsistent with the domestic decision of the House of Lords in *Harrow LBC v Qazi* [2004] 1 A.C. 983. The Court of Appeal declined, however, to follow *Connors* on the basis that the domestic rules of precedent and *stare decisis* require lower courts to follow the decisions of higher courts, and it is solely for the House of Lords to overrule *Qazi* on the basis of the decision in *Connors*.

BOOK THREE
PROCEDURE

CHAPTER 43

THE STATEMENT OF CASE

Substitute in line 8 of the paragraph CPR r.2.3(1) for CPR r.2.3(ii). **43–001**

2. PARTICULARS OF CLAIM

Add at the end of the paragraph: In *David Robert Green & Anor v* **43–004**
Alexander Johnson (A Firm) & Anor [2005] EWCA Civ 775, June 28, in which
the defendant appealed against an award of damages assessed as the diminution in value of the claimant's interest in a block of flats attributable to the
defendant's negligent advice to acknowledge the validity of two leases,
Carnwath L.J. made the observation at para.21:

> "It is essential in cases of this kind that each party should make clear in
> the pleadings, or at least before the hearing, precisely what bases of
> assessment it seeks to advance, and that the expert evidence if any
> should be clearly directed to the bases that are going to be put forward.
> If that is not done, there will be a danger of the issues becoming con-
> fused at the hearing, and a temptation to pick and choose different
> strands of valuation material in order to construct a new case, which
> may have superficial attractions but is not properly supported by
> coherent evidence."

There are only two natural occasions on which the preferred basis of assessment could be expressed: in the pleadings and in any skeleton argument.
Since expert evidence will be required in relation to such matters as diminution in value, it would not be satisfactory for the expression of any preference
to be left as late as a party's skeleton argument, served no doubt only days
before the trial. The right place in which to set out a case on loss is surely the
pleading. Carnwath L.J.'s requirement for a properly particularised pleading
on loss is both practical and, if adopted as the general rule, would be highly
advantageous to all concerned.

(1) General and special damage

(c) Particularity and particulars of special damage

43–018 Insert a new note at the end of the first sentence of the paragraph:

Note 71a: See *North Star Shipping Limited & Anor v Sphere Drake Insurance Plc & Anor* [2004] EWHC 2457 (Comm), October 27; [2005] Lloyd's Rep. I.R. 404; for an example of a case in which a claim for sue and labour expenses fell victim to an accusation of insufficient particularity. The pleading set out neither the measures relied upon or the facts relied upon in support of the proposition that those measures were reasonable, nor the cost of the measures. Permission to make a very belated amendment was, unsurprisingly, refused.

Add at the end of the paragraph: For those claims to which the range of Pre-Action Protocols applies, the risk of a defendant being left with insufficient information from which to comprehend and, therefore, to evaluate the claim against him should be heavily reduced. In personal injury cases, for example, para.3 of the applicable Pre-Action Protocol stipulates that the letter of claim shall contain an indication of the nature of any injuries suffered and of any financial loss incurred. Furthermore, "sufficient information should be given in order to enable the defendant's insurers/solicitor to put a broad valuation on the risk". The claimant is also to send the defendant as soon as practicable a schedule of special damages with supporting documents. In *Price v Price* [2003] 3 All E.R. 911, CA the Court of Appeal made clear the potentially dire consequences for a claimant who fails to give particulars of his special damages claims when asked to do so. Because of a difficulty in procuring supportive medical evidence, the claimant failed during the protocol stage to indicate the nature of his injuries or the financial loss he claimed to have incurred. No notice was given of any claim for loss of earnings. After issue of the claim form, the claimant again failed to provide details of his special damages claims, an omission eventually remedied 15 months after service of the proceedings. Reluctantly granting the claimant an extension of time for service of the long overdue particulars of claim, the Court of Appeal restricted recovery to those heads of claim which could be substantiated by medical evidence in existence at the date the claim form was issued.

Insert a new sub-heading and new paragraph after para.43–027:

(7) Periodical payments

43–027A There is now an additional requirement in claims for personal injury arising from the introduction of periodical payment orders under s.2 of the Damages Act 1996. New CPR, r.41.5 states:

"(1) In a claim for damages for personal injury, each party in its statement of case may state whether it considers periodical payments or a lump sum is the more appropriate form for all or part of an award of damages and where such statement is given must provide relevant particulars of the circumstances which are relied on.

(2) Where a statement under paragraph (1) is not given, the court may order a party to make such a statement.

(3) Where the court considers that a statement of case contains insufficient particulars under paragraph (1), the court may order a party to provide such further particulars as it considers appropriate."

Rule 41.5 empowers a court, where a statement under para.(1) is not given, to order a party to make such a statement. Equally where the court considers that a statement of case contains insufficient particulars under para.(1), it may order a party to provide such further particulars as it considers appropriate. Thus, when the pleadings first come to be reviewed (presumably for the purposes of allocation) there is an obligation on the judge to consider whether the absence of any reference to the form of award sought should be remedied, and if a form of award is specified, whether it has been properly thought through. Although the Practice Direction which supplements CPR, Pt 41 does not specify what has to be pleaded, this must logically include those matters specified in para.1 of the Practice Direction, being the so-called factors to be taken into account in the circumstances identified in r.41.7. For parties who feel unable to answer these difficult questions, there is to be no ultimate escape. CPR, r.41.6 obliges the court to consider and indicate to the parties as soon as practicable whether periodical payments or a lump sum award is likely to be the more appropriate form for all or part of an award of damages.

These new provisions, requiring in effect that a party's case as to the appro-   **43–027B**
priateness of periodical payments be set out in their pleadings, create an interesting conflict within judicial thinking. As stipulated in para.1 of the Practice Direction supplementing CPR, Pt 41, one of the considerations to which the court shall have regard when deciding to make a periodical payments order is the "nature of any financial advice received by the claimant when considering the form of award". Since financial advice would appear to be essential in order to determine the relative advantages of periodical payments as against a lump sum award, a claimant will inevitably need to obtain such advice. As the claimant will want to plead their desire for an order in the particulars of claim and will have to provide proper particulars of the reasoning for their preference, they will need to obtain financial advice before commencing proceedings. Such a need sits ill with the Court of Appeal's decisions in *Page v Plymouth Hospitals NHS Trust* [2004] EWHC 1154 (QB), May 20; [2004] Lloyd's Rep. Med. 337 and *Eagle v Chambers* [2004] EWCA Civ 1033, July 29; [2005] P.I.Q.R. Q p.18 to the effect that a claimant cannot recover the cost of obtaining financial advice on investment and management of their damages. This is yet another element of "front loading", whereby the onus of expenditure is laid upon a claimant at a time when the prospects of making any recovery will be unclear.

CHAPTER 44

THE TRIAL

I. PROOF

2. EVIDENCE

(1) General damage

(a) Damage inferred and damage presumed

44–008   Add at the end of the paragraph: In the conjoined appeals of *Jameel & Anor v Wall Street Journal Europe SPRL* [2005] EWCA Civ 74, February 3; [2005] E.M.L.R. 17, p.377, and *Dow Jones & Co Inc v Yousef Abdul Latif Jameel* [2005] EWCA Civ 75, February 3; [2005] E.M.L.R. 16, p.353, the defendants to libel proceedings sought to attack the twin propositions (i) that once defamation is proved, damage is presumed and (ii) that a claimant does not have to allege or prove special damage in order to establish a cause of action in defamation. Among the array of contentions advanced, all ultimately unsuccessful, the defendants argued that the presumption of damage was not compatible with Article 10 of the European Convention on Human Rights, Article 10 being said to preclude a claimant from relying on any legal presumption of damage to establish standing, injury or harm. Giving the judgment of the court in both cases, Lord Phillips M.R. rejected the defendants' argument but, in so doing, hinted at a qualification to the presumption's universality. At para.40 of his judgment in *Dow Jones*, Lord Phillips M.R. said:

> "We accept that in the rare case where a claimant brings an action for defamation in circumstances where his reputation has suffered no or minimal actual damage, (the presumption) may constitute an interference with freedom of expression that is not necessary for the protection of the claimant's reputation. In such circumstances the appropriate remedy for the defendant may well be to challenge the claimant's resort to English jurisdiction or to seek to strike out the action as an abuse of process."

(2) Special damage

Insert a new note at the end of the paragraph: **44–013**

NOTE 47a: In *Collins Stewart Ltd & Anor v Financial Times Ltd* [2004] EWHC 2337 (QB), October 20; [2005] E.M.L.R. 5, a libel action, Tugendhat J. acceded to the defendant's application to strike out a claim quantified as the diminution in the claimant company's market value caused by the alleged libel, Tugendhat J. concluding that the formulation was far too uncertain as a valuation to be acceptable as a legal basis for assessing damages.

Add at the end of the paragraph: In *Chase International Express Ltd v*   **44–014**
McRae [2003] EWCA Civ 505; [2004] P.I.Q.R. P p.314, for want of sufficient evidence, the Court of Appeal overturned an award of £41,871.43 for future loss of earnings calculated on a multiplier/multiplicand basis substituting a "round sum" of £12,500 calculated in accordance with *Blamire v South Cumbria Health Authority* [1993] P.I.Q.R. Q p.1. In a short concurring judgment, Newman J. remarked on the necessity for evidence to support the claims advanced, observing at para.31:

> "If the method of preparation and presentation adopted in this case reflects a common circumstance in connection with personal injury cases in the district court it has, in my judgment, departed too far from the basic principle that a claimant must prove his case by evidence capable of supporting the conclusions to which the court is invited to come . . . Approaching a matter with a broad brush does not mean an absence of material is acceptable. The broad brush approach merely enables the court to do justice where there may be gaps in detail, which normally arise because of the character of the case under investigation."

Those inclined to regard the new regime introduced by the CPR as ushering out the rules of evidence or the burden of proof in civil proceedings should think again!

II. JUDGMENT

2. ASSESSMENT OF DAMAGES

(1) In general

(a) Need for lump sum award

Delete, on line 23 of the paragraph, "may be" and substitute "are".   **44–019**

Delete, on line 24 of the paragraph, "Bill, which is destined to become the Courts".

Insert the following new paragraphs before "As for the structured settlement" on lines 26 and 27 of the paragraph:

44–019A Section 100 of the Courts Act 2003 substitutes for the existing s.2 of the Damages Act three new sections, numbered 2, 2A and 2B. The new s.2 provides:

> "(1) A court awarding damages for future pecuniary loss in respect of personal injury —
>> (a) may order that the damages are wholly or partly to take the form of periodical payments, and
>> (b) shall consider whether to make that order.
>
> (2) A court awarding other damages in respect of personal injury may, if the parties consent, order that the damages are wholly or partly to take the form of periodical payments.
>
> (3) A court may not make an order for periodical payments unless satisfied that the continuity of payment under the order is reasonably secure."

While empowering the courts to make periodical payment orders, s.2 is silent as to the circumstances in which the courts are to do so. The new s.2A(1) states:

> "(1) Civil Procedure Rules may require a court to take specified matters into account in considering —
>> (a) whether to order periodical payments;
>> (b) the security of the continuity of payment;
>> (c) whether to approve an assignment or charge."

44–019B The process by which these highly important changes have been implemented has not been a glorious one. Sections 100 and 101 were initially to be brought into force by the Courts Act 2003 (Commencement No.9, Savings, Consequential and Transitional Provisions) Order 2005 (SI 2005/547). However, the latter Order was apparently the victim of a defect requiring its repeal before implementation and, for commencement purposes, it was replaced by the Courts Act 2003 (Commencement No.10) Order 2005 (SI 2005/910). This Order (and, for that matter, its imperfect ancestor) did no more than bring ss.100 and 101 into force on April 1, 2005. To discover to which proceedings the sections are to apply, it is necessary to turn to the Courts Act 2003 (Transitional Provisions, Savings and Consequential Provisions) Order 2005 (SI 2005/911), para. 11 of which stipulates:

> "The powers conferred by section 2(1) and (2) of the Damages Act 1996 shall be exerciseable in proceedings whenever begun."

44–019C In accordance with s.2A(1), the detailed provisions governing the making of a periodical payments order are contained in the new CPR, rr.41.4–41.10 and the attendant Practice Direction. Rule 41.5 deals with the need to plead the case and is therefore considered at para.43–027A, above. Material to the making of an order, r.41.7 provides:

"When considering —

(a) its indication as to whether periodical payments or a lump sum is likely to be the more appropriate form for all or part of an award of damages under rule 41.6; or
(b) whether to make an order under section 2(1)(a) of the 1996 Act,

the court shall have regard to all the circumstances of the case and in particular the form of award which best meets the claimant's needs, having regard to the factors set out in the practice direction."

The so-called factors are to be found in para.1 of the Practice Direction which states:

44–019D

"The factors which the court shall have regard to under rule 41.7 include

—

(1) the scale of the annual payments taking into account any deduction for contributory negligence;
(2) the form of award preferred by the claimant including —
  (a) the reasons for the claimant's preference; and
  (b) the nature of any financial advice received by the claimant when considering the form of award; and
(3) the form of award preferred by the defendant including the reasons for the defendant's preference."

As to the circumstances which will lead a court to make a periodical payments order, at this early stage in the gestation of the jurisdiction it is possible to say only one thing with any confidence. The court cannot make such an order where it is not satisfied that continuity of payment is reasonably secure in the terms required by s.2(3). Continuity of payment will only be secure in three situations; where payment is protected by a guarantee given under the Act; where payment is protected by a scheme under s.213 of the Financial Services and Markets Act 2000; where the source of payment is a government or health service body.

44–019E

It is necessary to say something about the three principal factors and two subsidiary factors identified in the Practice Direction. None of the factors is hugely prescriptive, nor could be, given the potential range of situations in which periodical payments orders may be sought. The implication of factor 1 is that the smaller the award (allowing for contributory negligence) the less persuasive the case for a periodical payments order. Factors 2 and 3 — the parties' preferences — speak for themselves and will no doubt vary from party to party, although it seems unlikely that a defendant insurer will ever favour a periodical payments order over the certainty and finality of a lump sum award. More interesting is subsidiary factor 2(b) — the nature of any financial advice received by the claimant when considering the form of award. CPR, r.41.5 permits a party in their statement of case to state whether they consider periodical payments or a lump sum is the more appropriate form for all or part of an award of damages and where such statements are

44–019F

given relevant particulars of the circumstances which are relied on must also be provided. Fundamental to a party's selection will be financial advice on the relative advantages of the alternatives. It follows that every claimant will need to have addressed the relative advantages of periodical payments and therefore to have obtained financial advice before commencing their action. This is yet one further element in the increasing financial burden placed on a claimant in the pre-action stage. It remains to be seen if the cost of obtaining financial advice will be recoverable from the defendant.

44–019G   It is too early to offer much guidance from the courts on the combined operation of the factors. In *Louis Walton v Calderdale Healthcare NHS Trust* [2005] EWHC 1053 (QB), May 18, the parties had reached agreement on all heads of damage with the exception of the amount of compensation appropriate for care costs after the claimant attained the age of 19, it being agreed by the parties that such costs should be met by periodical payments. Silber J. nevertheless troubled to consider the factors which he spoke of at para.11 thus:

> "Applying these principles to the facts of this case, each of those factors supports the claimant's contention that there should be periodical payments for future care for the claimant after he has reached the age of 19 as the litigation friend and mother of the claimant strongly supports periodical payments on the basis of advice she has received from an Independent Financial Advisor. She explains in her second witness statement that she is concerned that as the claimant will live for another 70 or so years, if he was not to receive periodical payments, he might otherwise run out of capital and income which could pay for his care costs. I regard this as a cogent and sensible point as is the fact that a lump sum payment might not be large enough to compensate the claimant if there was to be a high rate of inflation in the future. I did not understand the defendants to oppose an order for periodical payments for the claimant's care. So after considering all the matters to which I have referred, I propose to make an order that the claimant's care costs after the age of 19 are to be paid by periodical payments."

Silber J.'s reliance upon the risk of a lump sum award being insufficient is not entirely logical. It might be thought that a lump sum award for the cost of future care, calculated taking a multiplier which reflected the claimant's age and life expectancy, would provide a fund sufficient to meet the claimant's care costs. Presumably, and such is not apparent from the judgment, there was some debate about the claimant's life expectancy. The balance of Sibler J.'s analysis is hardly open to objection and seems likely to anticipate the general trend of judicial thinking in such cases.

44–019H   The new s.2B gives the Lord Chancellor a power to enable courts to vary periodical payments under specified circumstances. The section provides:

> "(1) The Lord Chancellor may by order enable a court which has made an order for periodical payments to vary the order in specified circumstances (otherwise than in accordance with section 2(5(d)).

(2) The Lord Chancellor may by order enable a court in specified circumstances to vary the terms on which a claim or action for damages for personal injury is settled by agreement between the parties if the agreement —

(a) provides for periodical payments, and

(b) expressly permits a party to apply to a court for variation in those circumstances.

(3) An order under this section may make provision—

(a) which operates wholly or partly by reference to a condition or other term of the court's order or of the agreement;

(b) about the nature of an order which may be made by a court on a variation;

(c) about the matters to be taken into account on considering variation;

(d) of a kind that could be made by Civil Procedure Rules or, in relation to Northern Ireland, rules of court (and which may be expressed to be with or without prejudice to the power to make those rules)."

A different scheme of implementation applies to the power to vary, implemented by the Damages (Variation of Periodical Payments) Order 2005 (SI 2005/841), made on March 18, 2005 and coming into force, according to para.1(1), on the 14th day after the day on which it was made and, thus, on April 1, 2005. By contrast with the power to make a periodical payments order, para.1(5) of the Variation Order provides: "This Order applies to proceedings begun on or after the date on which it comes into force."

Two implementation regimes therefore coexist. The power to make a periodical payments order applies to all proceedings whether extant on April 1, 2005 or issued thereafter. By contrast, the power to vary applies only to claims commenced after April 1, 2005. Existing claims are safe from the effects of s.2B.

Addressing the power to make variable orders, para.2 of the Damages **44–019I** (Variation of Periodical Payments) Order states:

"If there is proved or admitted to be a chance that at some definite or indefinite time in the future the claimant will —

(a) as a result of the act or omission which gave rise to the cause of action, develop some serious disease or suffer some serious deterioration, or

(b) enjoy some significant improvement in his physical or mental condition, where that condition has been adversely affected as a result of that act or omission, the court may, on the application of a party, with the agreement of all the parties, or of its own initiative, provide in an order for periodical payments that it may be varied."

44–019J   Para.5 addresses the approach to be adopted when making a variable order, which it describes as follows:

> "Where the court makes a variable order —
>   (a) the damages must be assessed or agreed on the assumption that the disease, deterioration or improvement will not occur;
>   (b) the order must specify the disease or type of deterioration or improvement;
>   (c) the order may specify a period within which an application for it to be varied may be made;
>   (d the order may specify more than one disease or type of deterioration or improvement and may, in respect of each, specify a different period within which an application for it to be varied may be made;
>   (e) the order must provide that a party must obtain the court's permission to apply for it to be varied, unless the court otherwise orders.

44–019K   Para.10 addresses the variation procedure which is to be initiated by "an application for permission to apply for a variable order to be varied". The latter application, so para.10 informs us, must be accompanied:

> "by evidence —
>   (a) that the disease, deterioration or improvement specified in the order or agreement has occurred, and
>   (b) that it has caused or is likely to cause an increase or decrease in the pecuniary loss suffered by the claimant."

The respondent to the application then has 28 days to serve written representations on the strength of which the court will deal with the application without a hearing. If permission to apply is granted, the court must give directions, including directions as to the date by which the application for variation must be served and filed and the service and filing of evidence. No appeal lies from an order granting permission to apply.

44–019L   The mechanism, as will be seen, is a cumbersome amalgam of the administrative and the judicial. Who is to decide the application for permission to apply for a variation is not expressly stated. Given the timescale over which a periodical payments order may be expected to endure this is not likely to be the original trial judge. Even if it is, the judge will not realistically have any recollection of the issues in the case. There is no guidance as to the principles applicable to the grant of permission to apply. The reasonable inference must be that the threshold for obtaining permission to apply will not be vertiginous, leaving to the respondent at any oral hearing the opportunity to put straight irregularities which may have affected the grant of permission on paper.

It is doubtful if the power to order a variation will be of any real value. The **44–019M** obvious weakness of the scheme is its restriction to changes in the claimant's condition, physical or mental. There seems to be no reason why this should be the only change of circumstances acknowledged. Variation has no practical attractions for a defendant who will not want to expend money on a potentially open-ended review of the claimant's progress against the slim chance that some improvement may occur. There is no mechanism for a defendant to be kept informed of a claimant's progress so as to alert the defendant to an improvement. No claimant is ever likely to volunteer a variation where conditions have improved. The claimant can only make one application to vary and only then in respect of pre-ordained mental or physical conditions. Variation is not intended to address other matters known at the time the initial periodical payments order is made. Thus, for example, the mere escalation in the cost of care would not form the basis for an application to vary. The course of medical conditions capable of being identified when the original order is made is itself surely likely to be eminently predictable and therefore equally capable of being addressed in the main order, thereby excluding the possibility of an application to vary based upon them. In short, the power to vary looks to be an unwieldy tool, the plying of which will engender the same sort of unhappy satellite litigation as has been generated by the equivalent regime in ancillary relief proceedings. For further discussion see paras 35–018E and 35–018F.

Under the new s.2(8) of the Damages Act 1996, an order for periodical **44–019N** payments is to be treated as providing for the amounts to vary with the retail price index (although, by s.2(9), this provision may be disapplied or modified). For long-term medical care and treatment, this is less than satisfactory since it is well known that earnings inflation is greater than retail price inflation and that health care inflation, which reflects the earnings of the carers, is greater still. See further para.35–017 of the main text and para.35–018H, above.

The introduction of periodical payments brings with it a host of practical **44–019O** difficulties. Not least of these is the operation of CPR, Pt 36. By the Civil Procedure (Amendment No.3) Rules 2004 (SI 2004/3129), a new Rule, numbered 36.2A, has been inserted, applicable to personal injury claims for future pecuniary loss, and three new paragraphs have been added to existing Rules (para.36.10(3A) — offers to settle before commencement; para.36.20(1)(c) — costs consequences where the claimant fails to do better than a Pt 36 offer or a Pt 36 payment; para.36.23(4A) — allowance for deductible benefits). The new r.36.2A provides:

"(1) This rule applies to a claim for damages for personal injury which is or includes a claim for future pecuniary loss.
(2) An offer to settle such a claim will not have the consequences set out in this Part unless it is made by way of a Part 36 offer under this rule, and where such an offer is or includes an offer to pay the whole or part

of any damages in the form of a lump sum, it will not have the consequences set out in this Part unless a Part 36 payment of the amount of the lump sum offer is also made.

(3) . . .

(4) A Part 36 offer to which this rule applies may contain an offer to pay, or an offer to accept —

    (a) the whole or part of the damages for future pecuniary loss in the form of—

        (i)   either a lump sum or periodical payments, or

        (ii) both a lump sum and periodical payments,

    (b) the whole or part of any other damages in the form of a lump sum.

(5) A Part 36 offer to which this rule applies —

    (a) must state the amount of any offer to pay the whole or part of any damages in the form of a lump sum;

    (b) may state what part of the offer relates to damages for future pecuniary loss to be accepted in the form of a lump sum;

    (c) may state, where part of the offer relates to other damages to be accepted in the form of a lump sum, what amounts are attributable to those other damages;

    (d) must state what part of the offer relates to damages for future pecuniary loss to be paid or accepted in the form of periodical payments and must specify —

        (i)   the amount and duration of the periodical payments,

        (ii) the amount of any payments for substantial capital purchases and when they are to be made, and

        (iii) that each amount is to vary by reference to the retail prices index (or to some other named index, or that it is not to vary by reference to any index); and

    (e) must state either that any damages which take the form of periodical payments will be funded in a way which ensures that the continuity of payment is reasonably secure in accordance with section 2(4) of the Damages Act 1996 or how such damages are to be paid and how the continuity of their payment is to be secured."

The new provision concludes with the welcome constraint that a claimant will only be able to accept an offer as a whole and not merely accept those parts of it which immediately appeal.

44–019P   As provided for in new r.36.20(1)(c), in a claim to which r.36.2A applies, where a claimant fails to obtain a judgment "which is more advantageous than the Part 36 offer made under that rule", the court will order the claimant to pay any costs incurred by the defendant in the usual way. The new Rule does not achieve for periodical payments cases the costs certainties available in all other claims. Whether or not an award is more or less advantageous than a prior offer will be an entirely subjective judgment since one of the possible advantages (or, indeed disadvantages) of any award will be the inclusion or the exclusion of periodical payments. One way of mitigating the unpredictability of the outcome on costs may be to hold the parties to their pleaded cases on the virtues and vices of periodical payments so preventing the opportunist claimant who has not favoured a periodical payments order from subsequently claiming that the order achieved including provision for periodical payments is more beneficial than a rejected lump sum offer. But this is hardly to replicate the certainty or to mimic the tactical advantages of the Pt 36 regime in other cases. Reducing the risk in costs will inevitably release the parties to pursue their disputes to trial more freely since there will be a reduced incentive to settle.

44–019Q Commence this paragraph at "As for the structured settlement" on lines 26 and 27 of para.41–019 in the main text and continue as in the text of that paragraph.

Substitute for the last two sentences of this paragraph which is now para.44–019Q and was in the main text para.44–019: Adopting the recommendations of the Working Party, the new Practice Direction on structured settlements supplementing CPR, Pt 40 provides that parties should raise the question of a structured settlement in respect of future loss with the court during case management in every case where future loss is likely to equal or exceed £500,000 and in any other case where a structured settlement might be appropriate. The reasonable cost of financial advice from an independent financial adviser or accountant and any reasonably necessary advice from a party's medical and legal advisers is to be regarded as a cost in the litigation. In every case where there is a claim in respect of a child or patient, the parties or their representatives must put before the court advice as to the general desirability and appropriateness of the claimant entering into a structured settlement.

(b) Postponement of awards

Insert a new paragraph after para.44–021:

44–021A In *Adan v. Securicor Custodial Services Limited* [2004] EWHC 394 (QB), February 23; [2005] P.I.Q.R. P p.79, the claimant, who was in custody pending trial and subsequently sentenced to a lengthy term of imprisonment, sustained a brain injury in a collision while being driven to a court hearing by the defendant. Liability for the claimant's injury was admitted and a claim was made for the cost of the claimant's future special needs in the community. However, the claimant conceded that no such expenditure would be incurred in the foreseeable future because of his detention at Her Majesty's pleasure. The expert medical evidence agreed that it was possible in the future for the claimant to achieve semi-independent living in the community if his condition improved but no assessment of the chances could presently be made. Accordingly, the claimant argued that the issue of care and accommodation should be postponed indefinitely against the possibility of him one day returning to life within the community, relying on CPR, r.3.1(2) and Burton J.'s decision in *A v National Blood Authority* [2002] Lloyd's Rep. Med. 487 to support his argument. Eady J. held that, while the claim for accommodation and care could be characterised as a "question or issue" within CPR, r.3.1(2), the claim had to be considered in the context of the overriding objective which required cases to be dealt with fairly and expeditiously. Granting the claimant's application to adjourn determination of the claim would expose the defendant's insurers to an uncertain liability for an indefinite period which would be oppressive and undesirable. Eady J. added at para.23:

> "It is possible, no doubt, to envisage a hypothetical case where the nature of the damage and the likelihood that it will be incurred is clear, but quantification cannot yet be meaningfully assessed. In such a case, it may well serve the interests of all concerned to postpone the quantification until the necessary evidence becomes available. Here, by contrast, the prospect of any significant improvement in the claimant's mental health is largely speculative . . . it is not merely uncertainty as to quantifying an established head of loss that arises in this case. . . accordingly, it seems to me that the continuing incubus of potential liability and the uncertainty confronting the defendant's insurers would be out of all proportion to any possible corresponding benefit to the claimant."

On Eady J.'s analysis, there is thus a distinction between proving and quantifying that loss. To benefit from r.3.1(2), a claimant must be able to discharge the burden of proving *some* loss and will not avoid the dismissal of a claim on the strength of mere expectation that a loss may become provable in the future.

(c) Breakdown of awards and separate awards

44–022   Add at the end of the paragraph: However, the court's enthusiasm for reducing all such claims to their smallest component parts is not unlimited. In *Willbye v Gibbons* [2004] P.I.Q.R. P p.227, CA the claimant was seriously injured in a road accident at the age of 12. Addressing claims for extra assistance with any future children she might have and for the claimant's own care in later life, the Court of Appeal held that this type of future care claim should not be divided into discrete heads of damage. In making an assessment, said Kennedy L.J. at *ibid.*, para.16:

> "all that can realistically be done is to increase to some extent the fund available to the appellant to satisfy her need for assistance in the future, recognising the possible ways in which the demands may be made upon that fund, but not attempting to evaluate separate types of potential demand, because if potential demands are separately evaluated it may well turn out that there is duplication, or that substantial awards are made in respect of contingencies which have never happened."

Insert a new note at the end of the paragraph: **44–023**

NOTE 10a: For another example of separate awards see *Design Progression Limited v Thurloe Properties Ltd* [2004] EWHC 324 (Ch); [2004] 1 E.G.L.R. 121, a landlord and tenant case in which the defendant landlord had breached its statutory duty to respond in a reasonable time to the tenant's application for permission to assign his lease. Citing and relying upon paras 11–011 and 11–032 to 11–045 of the current edition of this work, Peter Smith J. found that the intention behind the defendant's failure to respond had been to extract a profit. While the defendant's design had ultimately proved unsuccessful, merely because the defendant's design had failed did not mean that it was not appropriate to award exemplary damages. Said Smith J.:

> "The calculation of the exemplary damages is not to be done by nice legal principles. It is to be assessed by an appropriate amount, having regard to the general criteria summarised above, to mark the displeasure of the Court of the defendant's conduct."

He went on to assess damages by reference to the profit the defendant would have made, had its design been successful, awarding the claimant £25,000.

Insert new paragraphs after para.44–023:

The Court of Appeal's decision in *Borders (UK) Limited & Others v   **44–023A** Commissioner of Police of the Metropolis & Anor* [2005] EWCA Civ 197, March 3, is an example of the maxim that hard cases make bad law. The claimant booksellers claimed both compensatory and exemplary damages from the defendant, memorably described by Sedley L.J. as a literary Fagin, for the systematic sale of vast numbers of books stolen from the claimants over an extended period. The claimants recovered compensatory damages of £279,594.89 and a separate award of £100,000 by way of exemplary damages. On the defendant's appeal, referring to the award of exemplary damages, Sedley L.J. acknowledged that:

> "if this part of the claim had been framed as a further claim for compensatory damages, it is evident from the Master's findings that it would have succeeded. Indeed it is evident that while Master Leslie had no difficulty in quantifying this element of the claim as part of the claimants' losses, he had rather more difficulty in characterising it as exemplary damages."

The exemplary damages claimed were in reality but a second component of the claimants' actual loss and therefore of the compensatory claim, merely languishing under an assumed identity. Driven by undeniable merits, the Court of Appeal was nevertheless unanimously prepared to uphold an award of exemplary damages since exemplary damages would be appropriate in the circumstances of the defendant having acted with a view to profit. With customary intellectual elegance, Sedley L.J. acknowledged that his decision had:

"to make up in justice what it lacks in logic; but the want of logic arises from a long-recognised anomaly in the law, and the justice of the outcome may assist in resolving it."

It is difficult to see quite how the Court of Appeal's decision will serve to resolve anomalies, whatever they may be. The better solution, to which Sedley L.J. seems to have been briefly attracted, would have been to require the claimants to re-plead their claim. See the case further at para.11–027A.

44–023B   Another interesting case is *Reventhi Shah v Kelly Anne Gale* [2005] EWHC 1087 (QB), May 27, the facts of which are exceptional. The claimant as executrix of her son's estate brought proceedings against the defendant claiming damages for the defendant's part in mistakenly directing a band of assailants in search of a different man to the claimant's son's address, where the assailants proceeded to attack and kill her son. The claim was for damages for assault and battery including a claim for aggravated damages but excluding a claim for pain and suffering. Clearly perplexed by the way in which the claim was framed, but citing para.37.001 of this work, Leveson J. awarded the claimant £750 for the assault and a separate sum of £2,000 by way of aggravated damages.

44–024   NOTE 26: Add at the end of the Note. *Williams v Devon CC* is now reported at [2003] P.I.Q.R. Q p.68, CA.

(2) Assessment where the action does not proceed to trial

(b) Judgment by default

44–029   Insert a new note in line 5 after reference to CPR, r.12.5(2):

NOTE 40a: The expression "specified amount of money" used in the Rule has a wider meaning than the older term "liquidated damages". Under the new rubric, it is possible for a claimant in a road traffic claim not involving personal injury to claim as damages the cost of repairs to a vehicle, specifying the cost of the repairs in the claim form and then to enter a default judgment for the amount of the damages claimed, thereby avoiding a disposal hearing.

(3) Assessment where there are several defendants

(a) Where all or some of the defendants default

44–031   Insert a new note at the end of the paragraph:

NOTE 44a: In *Yates v Elaby Trading as United Property Management & Moss*, unreported, November 17, 2003, Mitting J. held that where a claim was brought in the alternative, the court not only has the power under CPR, r.12.8(2)(b) not to enter default judgment against one defendant but has the duty not to do so.

APPEALS

II. APPEALS FROM AN AWARD OF DAMAGES BY A JUDGE

1. POWER TO REASSESS THE DAMAGES

Add at the end of the paragraph: The significance of the linguistic change **45–024** from rehearing to review applicable to appeals to the Court of Appeal at the end of a trial was given careful consideration by the Court of Appeal in *Assicurazioni Generali SpA v Arab Insurance Group* [2003] 1 W.L.R. 577, the Court of Appeal holding that the approach of the Court of Appeal when conducting a "review" of a decision below pursuant to CPR, r.52.11(1) should be the same as that formerly adopted by the Court of Appeal when conducting a "rehearing" pursuant to RSC Ord.59, r.3(1). The Court of Appeal observed that, in such cases, the older rehearing had been a rehearing only in a very specialist sense, Ward L.J. adding at *ibid.*, para.195:

> "When the Court of Appeal heard appeals on questions of fact the court was essentially conducting a review of the findings made by the judge below in as much as the Court of Appeal examined that judgment in the light of the evidence which had been presented to the court below without (save exceptionally) hearing evidence in this court. Mr Boyd submits that the change of language compels a different approach to be adopted. I do not agree. Our task is essentially no different from what it was — we consider the judgment testing it against the evidence available to the judge and we ask, as we used to ask, whether it was wrong. The Court of Appeal can only interfere if the decision of the lower court was wrong and in deciding whether or not findings of fact were wrong, we take a retrospective look at the case and do not decide it afresh untrammelled by the judge's conclusion . . . Bearing these matters in mind, the appeal court conducting a review of the trial judge's decision will not conclude

that the decision was wrong simply because it is not the decision the appeal judge would have made had he or she been called upon to make it in the court below. Something more is required than personal unease and something less than perversity has to be established."

In *Thomson v Kvaerner Govan Ltd* [2004] P.I.Q.R. P p.72, HL the House of Lords considered the proper approach of an appellate court to a decision on fact by a court of first instance. The House held that the proper approach was for the appellate court to ask itself whether it was in a position, not having the privileges of the judge who tried the case, to come to a clear conclusion that the trial judge was plainly wrong. In *Yorkshire Water Services Ltd v Taylor Woodrow Construction Northern Limited & Others* [2005] EWCA Civ 894, July 19, May L.J. addressed the meaning of CPR, r.52.11. He said:

"Rule 52.11 of the CPR provides that every appeal will be limited to a review of the decision of the lower court unless a practice direction makes different provision for a particular category of appeal . . . There has been judicial consideration about what under the CPR constitutes a review and what a rehearing. In truth, there is a spectrum shaded between the one and the other . . ."

2. GROUNDS FOR REASSESSING THE DAMAGES

(1) Error of law

45–027   Add at the end of the paragraph: The Court of Appeal's decision in *Chase International Express Ltd v McRae* [2003] EWCA Civ 505; [2004] P.I.Q.R. P p.21 may be regarded as an example of an award of damages being over-turned for error of law. The deputy district judge had awarded the claimant £41,871.43 as damages for future loss of earnings calculated using a multi-plier/multiplicand approach. Kennedy L.J. considered there to be insufficient evidence to enable the judge to employ the multiplier/multiplicand method-ology, displaced a multiplier/multiplicand in favour of a "round sum" calcu-lated in accordance with *Blamire v South Cumbria Health Authority* [1993] P.I.Q.R. Q p.1 and reduced the award for future loss of earnings to £12,500.

(2) Entirely erroneous estimate

(b) Where the measure of damages is more fixed

45–035   Add at the end of the paragraph: The ever greater reduction of awards to their component parts can create difficulties of its own. In *Willbye v Gibbons* [2004] P.I.Q.R. P p.227, the claimant, who had suffered a brain injury in a road traffic accident when a child, was awarded a lump sum of £45,000 for any additional care relating to future children and £60,000 for the extra future care in the final quarter of her life. Setting aside those awards, the Court of Appeal held that such claims should not be divided into discrete heads of damage because if potential demands were separately evaluated it might well turn out that there was duplication or that substantial awards were made in respect of contingencies that never occurred. The preferred approach was to increase the total future care award, Kennedy L.J. increasing an award in respect of future care from £136,932.16 to £181,129.60 broadly to reflect the two individual contingencies countenanced.

Add at the end of the paragraph: The preference for brackets is illustrated **45–040** by two recent decisions. In *Giambrone v JMC Holidays Ltd* [2004] 2 All E.R. 891, CA the claimants all suffered gastroenteritis or similar illnesses arising out of breaches of their contracts with the defendant while on holiday in Majorca. In each of the claims under appeal (selected as test cases) the trial judge had made an award for gratuitous care provided by relatives at a set rate of £50 per week. Having disposed of the defendant's appeals against the trial judge's awards, Brooke L.J. took it upon himself to encourage representatives of claimants and defendant to agree a guideline tariff for similar cases founded around the trial judge's award of £50 per week "so that the disproportionate cost of proving these small heads of damage may be avoided". In *Virgo Fidelis Senior School v Boyle* [2004] I.R.L.R. 268 the Employment Appeal Tribunal directed that guidelines laid down by the Court of Appeal on levels of compensation for injury to feelings in awards to employees subjected to race or sex discrimination should also be applied to compensation for injury to feelings awarded to whistle-blowers who had been subjected to a detriment by their employers because they had made a protected disclosure.